D1257261

REFLECTIONS ON
THE EPISTLES

By

J. W. C. WAND, D.D.

Treasurer of St. Paul's; formerly Bishop of London

LONDON
A. R. MOWBRAY & CO LTD

Printed in Great Britain by
A. R. Mowbray & Co Ltd in the City of Oxford
5442

First published in 1966

PREFACE

THE realistic temper of our day has led most commen-
tators to abandon the effort to find (except on a few
special occasions) a common theme running through the
collect, epistle and gospel of each Sunday. There seems
something to be said, therefore, for treating them as
separate entities.

So kind a reception was given to my *Reflections on the
Collects*, published last year, that I am encouraged to
issue a volume of *Reflections on the Epistles*. The difference
between the two is that, whereas the former 'reflections'
were original material, the latter have already appeared
in the columns of the *Church Times*, to which paper I am
grateful for permission to re-publish them. If the reception
given to this volume is equally encouraging, it is hoped
to publish a similar volume on the Gospels next year.

I should like to remind the reader that the book is not
meant to be read through as a continuing whole, but each
section is to be read, and if possible thought over,
separately. Of course each Epistle should first be read
from the Prayer Book before the reader turns to the
Reflection upon it.

✠ WM. WAND

1965

CONTENTS

REFLECTIONS ON
THE EPISTLES

THE DAY IS AT HAND

Advent Sunday   *Romans* 13. 8

THE authentic note of Advent is struck in to-day's epistle. 'The night is far spent, the day is at hand.'

This is no ordinary day. The note would be true enough if the immediate reference were the analogy of any dawn succeeding any night. But 'the day' in this instance has as much special significance as the Germans, before the First World War, used to instil into their phrase '*Der Tag.*'

The trumpet note of this day had sounded all down Hebrew history. It was originally the Day of the Lord, the day when Jehovah would undertake the final battle against his enemies, who were of course the enemies also of Israel. But Amos had shown that there were guilty ones among the Hebrews, both Israel and Judah, as well as among the heathen, and justice demanded that both alike should be punished. So the Day of the Lord, from being the day of victory, became the day of assize when the judgement would be set and the books opened and everyone, Jew and Gentile alike, would be judged according to his deeds.

Later the Day became the moment when the Kingdom would be ushered in and the reign of God established over all the earth. John the Baptist in his time proclaimed that this day was at hand and that the Kingdom was even at the doors. And Jesus preached that it had come in his own person.

*   *   *

The early Church never quite lost this sense of urgency. Its members soon learnt that the introduction of the Kingdom did not mean the immediate end of the world. The end-time might itself prove to be a long period and the final Day might be indefinitely postponed.

But the urgency was still there. The light of that dawn was like the lights of an oncoming car. They seem small and dim in the distance, but they approach more and more rapidly, increasing in volume and intensity as they come, until you are completely immersed in the whiteness. Only the light of eternity does not pass and lose itself in the dark.

Ever since the teaching of Jesus the Christian world has felt that it lived within the light of the approaching end. That end is not a chronological point in the distance: it is all about us. Any one point in time is as near eternity as any other. We live in the eternal sphere here and now.

That was the clear teaching of Jesus, especially as seen in the Fourth Gospel. 'This is life eternal, to know thee the only God and Jesus Christ whom thou hast sent.' Such a faith does not preclude a later seeing of God face to face, a time, a moment, when the veil of material things will fall away and we shall see him as he is.

*   *   *

In any case this note of urgency is intended to make us realize the essentials of our situation in the world, and take prompt action. The epistle is a summons to holiness of life. It begins and ends with the same point, and the call to awake out of sleep is inserted in the middle to make us realize the more strongly that this is not a matter for debate but for action.

Owe no man anything, but to love one another. Get out of your night-clothes, and into your battle-dress. No time for wantonness, but put on the Lord Jesus Christ— the words that were responsible for the final conversion of St. Augustine.

Care for one another: that is what we must do. No doubt we perform much of the task indirectly—through the amenities of the Welfare State, through the Government's plans for the distressed areas in the North, through all the schemes for the improved education of the rising generation. We thank God that to-day the nation begins to recognize its duties to all its members.

But that satisfaction is misplaced unless we are acting in the same spirit towards the individuals in our own immediate neighbourhood with whom we are in constant or occasional contact. Only 'he that loveth another hath fulfilled the law.'

THE WORD OF GOD

THERE are two phrases often used about the Bible which seem at first sight contradictory but which are capable, when properly interpreted, of expressing complementary truths. The one is 'The Bible is the Word of God,' the other 'The Bible is to be read like any other book.'

There can be no doubt that, for the Christian at least, the Bible is the Word of God. That is part of his fundamental belief: it has been the view of the Church in all its branches in all ages of its history. We mean by it a number of things. First, it is the Word of God speaking to us out of the silence of the centuries, telling us about himself and his purposes for the world he has made.

Then it is the record of that Word which was also his Son, the expression in actual personality of the Father's self-revelation. The Old Testament tells of the long preparation for the coming of that Word: the New Testament tells of his life upon earth as a man among men and records the immediate consequences of that life.

But also the Bible is the Word of God in the sense that in it God speaks to us here and now. Through it the Church gains continual guidance, and the individual soul receives comforting strength and illumination.

*   *   *

None of this should prevent the Bible from being read like any other book. This inspiration comes to us through words printed on paper by the same processes as are used in the production of any other book. The individual books of which the Bible is composed were written by human authors who no doubt went through the same pains of composition as those endured by any other author, although we may well believe that they received a special degree of guidance from the Holy Spirit of God.

Modern learning has shown us more clearly than any other age has been able to discern how the individual books composing the Bible were made up. We can see how various authors consciously improved upon each other, and how later editors made composite volumes out of a combination of their efforts.

Further, we have learnt how slowly the Church built up what we now know as the canon of Scripture, deciding which books alone should be regarded as fully authoritative. It is not until the middle of the fourth century, in the time of St. Athanasius, that we find the Church using a list precisely like our own.

Together with this knowledge of the way in which the Bible was gradually built up Christians have gone on accumulating treasures of knowledge about the background of Bible times, about the way in which its people used to live, and even about the characteristic ways in which they were taught to think. As a result we have come to view the Bible not as some fetish fallen down from heaven, but as the anthology of a nation from the time of its first foundation to its dissolution.

*   *   *

In the face of these two very different aspects of the sacred literature, how are we to use it in such a way as not to lose the value of either?

First we read the Bible in order to learn the record of God's self-revelation in history. We want to know what he tells us about himself. Obviously every detail about our Creator, Redeemer and Friend will be most precious. Whatever we can learn about the earthly and material circumstances in which this revelation was given will help to a fuller understanding.

Then we shall read it in order to understand the teaching given through the pens of inspired men about God, his Son, his Spirit and his ways here and now. Such knowledge is able to make us wise to the things of eternal life.

Finally we shall read it in order to catch the special word it has to say to our own soul. In joy or sorrow, birth or bereavement, sickness or health, elation or despondency there is always some word from God himself waiting for us in his holy Word. Those who read it often and know where to look in their hour of need are not likely to be disappointed.

THE MINISTRY

THE Greek Bible commonly uses two words for the sacred ministry. One, the favourite word in the Old Testament, is *leitourgia*, from which we get our word 'liturgy'; the other, the favourite word in the New Testament, is *diakonia*, from which we get our word 'deacon.'

As we shall see, it is possible to show differences in shades of meaning, but roughly the two words cover much the same ground. There is actually one phrase in which St. Paul unites them. He is talking about his collection for the saints in Jerusalem, and he speaks of it as 'the ministration of this service' (2 Cor. 9. 12).

In this case it is the word 'liturgy' that is translated by 'service.' It has the more exalted history of the two. In Greek circles it was used of some great service performed by a person of rank for the State, often at his own expense. In the Old Testament it is used of the service rendered in the worship of God by the priest. Even in the New Testament that use is continued, as for instance when St. Luke says that the priest Zacharias fulfilled the days of his 'ministry' or 'service,' otherwise his 'liturgy.'

In this exalted ministry the laity have their own part to play, as in the instance quoted from St. Paul, when it is extended to cover the giving of alms to one's fellow-men. But the word still carries with it the suggestion of a noble act, something which is directed in the first place to God himself.

*   *   *

The word *diakonia* has a much more humble origin. It applies to service of one's fellow-men in the ordinary circumstances of everyday life. It is used of household chores and particularly of the preparation for a meal. So St. Luke says that Martha 'was cumbered about much serving' when he means that she had to get the dinner ready.

This word, too, in spite of its humble origins, began to be used of ministerial office. One remembers how the apostles complained that they ought not to spend their time 'serving tables' when there was so much preaching to be done. Then the seven 'deacons' were appointed to take that task off their shoulders. Paul reckons such service as part of a regular 'diaconate' or ministry (*Rom.* 12. 7).

This then gives us a rather different view of the ministry as a function exercised not only towards God but also towards our fellow-men. It includes the humblest and most menial of tasks.

*   *   *

From the consideration of these two words several conclusions follow. We see first of all that ministry is a service performed both for God and man. It embraces all our surroundings physical and spiritual. It must be a very comfortable thought for any man that he is thus in happy correspondence with the whole of his environment.

The second conclusion is that this ministry is not the exclusive possession of any particular section of society. All of us alike are called to share in it. The priest has special functions to perform, but they are functions within the body of God's people. It is that body as a whole which is the ministering unit.

To this we must add, thirdly, that the *locus* of our ministry, the point at which we have to offer our service, is precisely where we are now. God may in due course call us to some new position, but at the moment, whether we are priest, nun, missionary, butcher, baker or candle-stick maker, we are expected to perform our service without delay exactly where we are.

Finally it follows that we serve God and man best by doing our allotted task to the best of our ability. Shoddy workmanship brings no credit either to the Master, the workman or the customer. We need not be afraid of this demand for the best. The Spirit of God enters our personality and gives grace for the performance of our task, not only to the ordained clergy but to everyone, clerical or lay, who relies upon him. We are all called by God, and he provides the means for an adequate response to his call.

REJOICE

TO-DAY'S epistle rings out its iterated note of joy, 'Rejoice, and again I say Rejoice.' The reason given is that the Lord is at hand.

In view of the way in which we generally interpret the teaching of Advent and illustrate it with our sombre penitential colours, this emphasis on joy may seem a little unexpected. There are indeed three special ways in which the Lord may be said to be on the point of 'coming': one is at the Last Day, when he comes to the whole world; the second at death, when he comes to the individual; and the third at Christmas, when we think of his coming as a babe at Bethlehem. Can they all be anticipated with equal joy?

The first is undoubtedly the sense in which St. Paul is using the term in this passage. He says with complete confidence that the Lord is at hand, and he evidently shared the belief of his fellow-Christians that the end of the world would not be long delayed.

It involved an agonizing re-appraisal of the situation when his contemporaries began to realize that the Lord delayed his coming. We can see how they learnt to balance their disappointment with fresh emphasis on the indwelling of his Holy Spirit, on his presence in the Eucharist, and on his existential appeal to each one whom he challenged to put his trust in him.

*   *   *

All these three 'comings' have their element of joy, although it is sometimes mingled with sterner feelings.

It is perhaps natural that we in our time should associate the special feeling of joy with the commemoration of our Lord's birth. We are reminded that this was the beginning of a new era in the history of mankind, which was meant to be characterized by a new and more intense happiness than any the world had hitherto experienced. That is certainly the feeling that we should hope to be uppermost among us at the Christmas festival.

But Paul wants much more than that: he expects the joy in the Lord's coming to be perennial. It is to be the dominant note of our lives. We Christians should be recognized as a specially happy people.

For this reason the Christian's rejoicing must always be 'with moderation.' In spite of the view that the kind of joy aroused by the thought of Christ's coming was expected to be of an ecstatic character, the fact that it was under control must be obvious to all men, especially to outside observers.

Such a thought may well be in our minds this Christmas, whether we remind ourselves of the hungry millions in other lands or of the death-toll upon the roads of our own country. Let our moderation be known to all men, so that life may be spared and the hunger of the starving be satisfied.

*　　　*　　　*

If we observe this caution, then for the rest we are to be without anxiety. One of the reasons why we have so little joy in our lives is that we are determined to take over the direction of them ourselves. We do not realize that by doing so we actually dishonour God. After all, he is in charge of us, and we have to learn to 'cast all our care upon him, for he careth for us.'

And this is true even with the world as it is. In spite of the many threats to peace, in spite of the troubles

B

through which our own country is passing, in spite of the thousand and one mishaps that meet us every day of our lives, in spite of all we are to be 'anxious in nothing.'

The remedy against such anxiety is simply to let God know what we want. It is not enough to say that he knows already. Of course he does, but like trustful children we must talk to our Father about it, and like normal children we shall be ready to thank him for what we have already received. It is in this mutual confidence that our happiness will largely consist.

If we thus recognize God's constant presence with us now and learn to rely upon it, we shall look forward with real joy to the moment when the veil is withdrawn and we see him face to face.

SPOKEN BY HIS SON

Christmas Day   *Hebrews* I. I

WE are sometimes told that God reveals himself, not in statements of abstract truth, but in his mighty acts. In that case the most revealing event in history was the birth at Bethlehem.

It was, of course, an event in time and place. The precise details of both have been disputed, but the central fact itself is accepted by every responsible scholar. It has not been found easy to fix it exactly on the chronological chart, but it has, nevertheless, become the event by which we date every other event.

However, it is not its position in time that gives to this event its importance, but the fact that it belongs not only to time but to eternity. It reveals God precisely because it includes an incursion from eternity into time.

The Babe, with no rational thoughts yet of its own, is the vehicle of expression for the mighty Reason that controls the stars and guides the planets in their courses. He represents, he is, an Incarnation. In him God has entered anew into his own creation. He has become the personal element in the being of one of his own subjects. He will reveal himself, but only in so far as such revelation is possible through the human nature of this Babe as it grows and develops into full manhood.

*   *   *

God as at this time gave his only-begotten Son to be born of a pure Virgin. But that does not exhaust the Christmas message. The collect for the day reminds us that we too are to become his children by adoption and grace.

For that we must be regenerate, born again. Our new birth means that Christ is born in us. That is the heart of the Christmas message. The Incarnation is not something that happened once and for all a long time ago in history. It is something that, having once happened, abides for ever. Nothing can change it. The Eternal Word is still united with the human nature of Jesus of Nazareth.

Being united with his, he can enter into ours. 'I in them and thou in me,' he once said, addressing his Father. As the Eternal Word is in Christ, so Christ is in us—with one exception. In Christ the Word was the personal element constituting the individuality of Jesus. In our case he united himself with *our* personality, strengthening *our* individuality but giving it the opportunity to be conformed to his own.

Thus, as the Son of God descending from heaven and becoming incarnate spoke to humanity through the life and teaching of Jesus of Nazareth, so we are expected to show the character of Jesus in our own thoughts, words and actions. As God expressed himself in Jesus; so Jesus would express himself in us.

*   *   *

The trouble is that, simple as it sounds, this task is really beyond our powers. It is an 'easy lesson hard to learn.' We have no difficulty in understanding what it says, but enormous difficulty in remembering it and acting upon it at the appropriate moment. It sounds so simple, when need arises, just to step mentally on one side and let Jesus do the required action for you. Yet, as anyone knows who has tried it, over and over again our own frailty intervenes and the effort defeats us.

That is why the collect insists on the need for daily renewal. To keep the human mind fresh and active requires continual reinvigoration. Jesus himself was fully aware of this aspect of human psychology, and for that reason promised the never-failing assistance of the Holy Spirit. Thus, 'being daily renewed by his holy Spirit,' we may the more easily be reminded of his presence within us and of his desire to seek self-expression through us.

All this is dramatized and reinforced in our Christmas Communion. He who was born in the stable at Bethlehem is in a very real sense born anew on our altars and in our hearts. All the tenderness and strength, the peace and good will, the general love and the particular affection that are his are aroused in us and wakened to expression by the influence of his Spirit upon our minds. The heart of Christmas is the Christmas in our hearts.

DEAR FATHER

AFTER all the jollity and excitement of Christmas Day and the subsequent holiday, Sunday gives us a chance of quiet reflection on the meaning of the history we have just commemorated. The gospel for the day retells the story in simple terms: the epistle gives the explanation. It is with the latter that we are concerned here.

The epistle describes in effect the different fortunes of two children, growing up together in the same contemporary household, the one a slave's son, the other the legitimate son of the master of the house. The slave is evidently a favoured one, for the two children are allowed to play together, and even to share the same tutor. They also submit to the same discipline. If a stranger saw them together, he would hardly distinguish the difference in their condition.

But, as they grow towards adolescence, their paths diverge. The one realizes that he is a member of the owner's family, the other that he is merely a chattel, in the eyes of the law not a person at all, but just a piece of property to be dealt with as the master wishes. Inevitably the psychology of the two changes. The one, as he grows to manhood, looks out upon the world with confidence: he is a member of the ruling race, and he will have a share in the ownership of what he surveys. The other begins to cringe with fear. He has no hope of any place or position of his own except at the caprice of his master: all that he can certainly expect is punishment if anything goes wrong.

At this point, however, there is seen a great difference in the Christian family. As the children have grown up together, the slave child has caught the spirit of the other. No sooner has he begun to recognize the divergence in their conditions than the filial affection of the other has proved too strong for him. He, too, has learned to cry 'Dear father.' Since the endearment comes from the heart the father accepts it, and receives the slave child by adoption into his own family. Henceforth the two boys work and play together without fear, sharing alike the freedom of the household.

Not so much of a fairy tale as it might appear, says the epistle; for the Christian that is just what has happened. He has been taken out of the sphere where he was under the domination of inexorable fate or of a hard, implacable law, and has been taken into a sphere of love and freedom in which he is recognized as God's son, as a freeman of his city, as a prince sharing the throne of the world with the Creator whom he now recognizes as Father.

*   *   *

This, it is implied, is the difference Christmas has made. God came down in the person of his Son to an enslaved world in order that men might be joined with that Son, filled with his spirit and set free to live his kind of life.

It is well known how Jesus in his teaching established the same position. Indeed he distinguished three periods or moments of our growth. First that of the servant or slave, whose business it is simply to obey orders. Second, that of the friend, whose privilege it is to know and understand the mind of the Master. And third, that of the Son, who has been adopted into the family and made co-heir with the Master's own son.

The moral of all this is clear. If we are sons, then we must live as members of the family: we must not betray the family or let it down. Since we have the Spirit of God in our hearts, crying 'Abba, Father,' we must show the character of God's children.

Christmas teaches us that we must live in love, in hope, in confidence. But it does more than that: it gives us the glad tidings that we have *power* thus to live. Christ who was born in the stable of Bethlehem, on our altars and in our hearts is the guarantee both of that power and of our success.

GRACE

Christmas II   2 *Corinthians* 8. 9

THERE is a never failing interest in the history and meaning of words. They develop a variety of uses while retaining an undertone of the application that first gave them birth. The clever writer achieves some measure of his charm by keeping that original meaning always in view.

Take, for instance, the word 'governor' which can be used for so many things, from a piece of machinery to the head of a state, and yet never quite loses its first significance of a helmsman or steersman. Or we can take the term we are expected to meditate upon to-day, the word 'grace.' There are few words that have so wide a variety of connotation and yet retain throughout some fragrance of their first association. It is good that we should recognize this, for 'grace' is one of the most important words in the Christian's vocabulary. At least one historian of the early mediæval period has said that the introduction of the idea of grace entirely changed the course of European history.

The essence of the idea is charm or favour, something pleasant that you cannot create for yourself. We get it in our phrase 'free, gratis and for nothing,' where the middle term is actually the word 'grace.' St. Paul uses it for anything from the loving-kindness of God to the collection for the saints at Jerusalem.

*   *   *

So in the shortest epistle in the liturgical year, we are reminded that we have had experience of the grace of our

Lord Jesus Christ, that, though he was rich, yet for our sakes he became poor. Here the word might very well be translated 'generosity,' the overflowing kindness that gives more than either we desire or deserve.

The real test of such generosity lies in the cost to the person who bestows it. Most of us are good-natured enough to give out of our abundance to someone with a particular need which it is well within our power to satisfy. But how few of us are willing to hand over to another something we really want for ourselves.

Yet our Lord Jesus Christ did more than that. He denuded himself of all the wealth of heaven. Though he was infinitely rich, he became infinitely poor—poor not merely in the lack of money or shelter but in the more positive sense of suffering and shame. We are reminded of the graphic phrase used elsewhere by St. Paul 'he emptied himself.'

And this he did, not for people who deserved well of him, as we may have given a Christmas present to a friend or faithful employee, but 'while we were yet sinners,' when indeed there was not one word to be said for us, so hopelessly had we failed to live up to our possibilities.

*   *   *

His gift to us was thus utterly free and undeserved. Even so we seldom realize how great it is. It is not some temporary benefit, some addition to our amenities, some extra ornament to the existing furniture of life. It is nothing less than himself—'his presence and his very self and essence all divine.' This is so great and mysterious a gift that we do not often dare to remind ourselves of it.

Yet the collect has the courage to call to mind the passage in 2 Peter 'that we may be made partakers of the divine nature.' It helps us to recall some phrases used by our Lord himself. 'I am the vine, ye are the branches.'

'I in thee and thou in me.' 'He that eateth this bread shall live for ever.'

Jesus thus gives himself, makes himself one with us, until we can say 'It is no longer I that live but Christ that liveth in me.'

This is the ultimate meaning of grace, that we in all our frailty may be united with the power that controls the universe.

THE FELLOWSHIP OF THE MYSTERY

EPIPHANY is the festival of revelation. On any show-ing revelation is the basic miracle. Apart from creation itself, it is the fundamental incursion of eternity into time.

It should involve a two-way traffic. If God reveals himself to us in time, we, by studying the things of time, ought to be able to find our way back to him in eternity. By admiring the beauty of the universe, by tracing the movement of history, by responding to the moral call of the conscience, we ought to learn to understand God and his ways.

Some scholars, however, will not accept this as revela-tion. They point out that each of these natural phenomena is capable of other explanation. What we need is some key to be given us direct by God which will open to us in a clear and authoritative manner the knowledge merely suggested by these natural means.

Such authoritative revelation Christians believe they have in their Bible.

*　　　*　　　*

In the Old Testament God is revealed in each of its formal divisions: the Law, the Prophets, and the Writings. In the Law God is understood through the demands he makes. When we do our shopping we reveal ourselves by the things for which we ask, and the man behind the counter ends up by knowing a good deal about us. In the Law God asks for two things from his people: first that they should worship him, and second that they should strive after moral goodness. So we know that God is the highest being in all existence, and that goodness is the very essence of his nature.

In the Prophets we find God revealing himself in the mighty acts of history. In the old division of the sacred writings the main historical books are grouped with the prophets. The reason is that prophets were the great interpreters of history. They made it their business to show not merely the ordinary course of events on the secular plane, but how in all of them the controlling hand of God could be seen. It is not Israel's greatness that is portrayed but the greatness of God. He is the one who delivered his people out of Egypt and Babylon. He is the deliverer, the Saviour.

In the third division, the Writings, which include books like the Psalms, Job, Proverbs and the Wisdom literature, we see God reflected as in a mirror by the character and conduct of his true worshippers. Here is laid down the proper attitude towards life and the world on the part of the righteous man, even to the details of daily conversation and manners. Here in this pattern of the godly life the nature of God is revealed. So in the Law, the Prophets and the Writings God is made manifest.

*   *   *

But the Old Testament offers only a partial, a preparatory revelation. The full epiphany is reserved for the New Testament, when God is made manifest in the person of his Son.

It is interesting that the first part of the New Testament to be written was intended to explain that revelation. Within twenty years of the Crucifixion St. Paul was writing his letters to instruct his converts more thoroughly in the faith they had adopted. Before another twenty were out men had begun recording their recollections of Jesus' own life and teaching. Thus ultimately we came into possession of our four Gospels, which in telling the story of Jesus explain how in his every word and act he revealed the character of God.

But the New Testament does not stop there. It is not satisfied until it has shown us how God continued to be revealed through the 'body' of his Son, which was the assembly of the faithful, the Church. As his physical body had been frail, so was the Church. But through its very imperfections the love of God was and is more precisely known. It will continue so to be until we see him face to face, and reach the final fullness of joy depicted in the book specifically known as the Manifestation or Revelation.

TRANSFORMED BY RENEWING

Epiphany I   *Romans* 12. 1

THE word 'epiphany' means appearance, and it is
applied particularly to the visible manifestation of
some divinity. That manifestation may be made either
in person or in some specially striking deed by which
the presence and power of the divinity is made known.

In the ancient world it was not uncommon to think
of such divine presence as being manifested in kings or
great officers of state. The close relations held to exist
between the Egyptian Pharaohs and the gods is well
known. In Syria the title Epiphanes, or God made
manifest, was actually adopted by the King Antiochus
who tried to compel the Jews to accept Greek customs
and so brought on the wars of the Maccabees.

In the Pastoral Epistles the word is used of both the
first and the second coming of Christ. There is one
particular passage (2 *Tim.* 1. 10) in which the term is
used precisely as we use it to-day. It speaks of the age-
long purpose of God 'which has now been made manifest
through the epiphany (the appearance on earth) of our
Saviour.'

*   *   *

In the feast of the Epiphany we celebrate the manifestation of Christ in particular to the Gentiles; and the story
of the Magi is taken as a specially appropriate illustration
of that theme. The feast of the Epiphany is really the
festival of the Christian revelation.

Since revelation is, after creation itself, the fundamental
miracle, that God should make himself known to man
requires that he should in some sense come out of eternity

into time. He must appear out of the sphere of being which is proper to himself in order to make himself known in the sphere that is proper to us. A line of communication must be thrown between the two types of existence, the human and the divine.

There is no reason why God should not in thus making himself known use ordinary, familiar, human means. He may speak to us in the voice of some honoured teacher, the smile of a beloved friend, the lingering light of sunset, the violence of a mountain storm. It is true that some scholars will not recognize this method as revelation in the true sense of the word, but that seems unreasonable.

It is well, however, to mark the distinction between a general and a special revelation. If what has just been described is a general revelation, then the special revelation, the only kind of revelation that some authorities will recognize, is that given through Christ, in the Bible and in the Church. Certainly in those latter instances we can see an epiphany, a manifestation, a revelation of God of a depth and an extent hardly possible in the other cases.

*   *   *

But the revelation, however given, is not appropriated without some effort on our part. In contrast with the Magi, who actually saw the infant Christ, we describe ourselves as those who 'know thee now by faith.' In other words, for a revelation to be of any value it must be received by us with open minds. There must be response to God's overture. We must be transformed by the renewing of our mind. Our whole attitude must be altered and ourselves with it.

Perhaps we respond so little because we do not understand the nature of the faith we are expected to display. Faith does not mean believing without evidence; still less does it mean believing what we know to be untrue! It means trusting such evidence as we have in spite of appearances to the contrary.

And who at such a time as this would wish to make any other choice? Surrounded by the tokens of God's love and with the emotions of the Christmas season still powerful within us, we are bound to look upon all other explanations of the universe and of our individual part in it as not only unsatisfying but foolish. The manifestation of Jesus and his love is still the epiphany which reveals with complete adequacy the nature of the Eternal.

CHRISTIAN CHARACTER

ST. PAUL is surprisingly practical. He is not only
the first great Christian theologian: he is also the
great exponent of Christian conduct. He is not content
to teach us what we ought to believe: he also tells us
how we ought to behave.

It has often been pointed out how he sets out in some
of his epistles, such as Ephesians, Colossians, 1 Timothy
and Titus, moral codes, or tables of manners, almost
as if he were a lecturer on ethics. It is rather more surprising that in his great doctrinal letter to the Romans
we should find him leading up to a detailed description
of the true Christian character. Since this exposition is
given as the Epistle for the second Sunday after Epiphany,
we are evidently expected by the Church to regard it as
a 'manifestation' or revelation of what we should strive
to become.

It is possible to discern three different sections in the
advice here given. The first is addressed to what one might
call the Christian leader, the man who recognizes that
he has a special gift and has begun to exercise it in his
ministry. 'Let us each one use our gifts to the full. If we
have been granted the ability to prophesy let us prophesy
to the limit of our faith. If welfare-work is our special
sphere, let us busy ourselves in the service of others. If
we are teachers, let us concentrate on teaching. If we are
preachers, let us inspire comfort and good counsel.'

*   *   *

This almost looks as if there were beginning to emerge
in the Christian community something like a professional

ministry. At least if development has not yet proceeded
so far, anyone who has discovered in himself some ministerial gift is urged to exercise it to the full.

The warning is against being half-hearted. If we have
any function to perform we must be sure to do it to the
utmost of our ability: nothing less than the best of our
energies will do. As we see from the next section, this
applies not only to the semi-professional gifts but to our
general character.

'If we are bestowing charity, we are to do it from a
wholly disinterested motive. If we are in a position of
authority, we must not be slack but show an example of
alertness. If we are visiting the sick, we must carry with us
an atmosphere of cheerfulness. We must be truly loving
without simulating an affection we do not feel. We must
set ourselves deliberately to hate evil and admire good.
We must try to cultivate real affection for the brethren.
We must try to obtain recognition for others rather than
for ourselves.'

All this is little more than a translation of St. Paul's
words. They come home to us with a new and fresh
meaning when conveyed in a modern idiom. The great
lesson they teach is that we are always to be on the look
out for opportunities of genuine service. This applies
whether we like people or not. We are not to pretend
to a sentimental fondness we do not feel. We are to do
our utmost to like people: but even where our affections
are not engaged, we are to do everything possible to make
ourselves truly helpful.

*   *   *

The combination of genuine sincerity with beneficent
purpose is intended to characterize the third class of whom
St. Paul speaks, those who have to recognize that religion
is not some pastime for leisure hours but a serious business.

It should dominate the whole order and purpose of our lives. 'He who sets about the profession of Christianity must be business-like, full of enthusiasm, optimistic, patient in adversity, keen about his prayers, willing to share his goods with needy brethren.'

It is an attractive picture of the Christian character. Those who attain it are, as Jesus said, the salt of the earth. 'Cultivate a ready sympathy both with the happy and with the miserable. Try to share in the common thoughts and aspirations of the rest. Don't be social climbers but associate with the humble.'

Here is a character expressive of a true Christianity, a 'coming-down' religion, a religion of Incarnation. It is an exposition of the character of the Incarnate in the terms of everyday life.

OVERCOME EVIL WITH GOOD

Epiphany III (St. Paul)   *Romans* 12. 16

ST. PAUL is the most important figure in early Church history in several respects, but in nothing more than as an interpreter of the teaching of Christ.

We have to remember in any case that his is the earliest written interpretation that we have. It is not presented to us in a formal treatise but in the shape of occasional letters, written in answer to the questions raised from time to time by his converts. And he was already writing those letters within twenty years of the Crucifixion.

We can see how much we owe to his interpretation if we compare it with that given in the Synoptic Gospels. They, of course, are not written in so explanatory a style. They consist mostly of narrative, and it is likely that, although they were composed after St. Paul's writing was over, they rely on different sources of information from those available to him. In any case it is extraordinary how little they betray any influence from him.

If we try to summarize the message of the Synoptic Gospels in general, we may be surprised to realize how intensely psychological it all is. Its emphasis is on the mind and the various attitudes of the mind. The one thing that Jesus seems to demand is faith. It is true that such faith must issue in right conduct and must face the judgment that is to mark the end of the world. But, throughout, it is the motive, the attitude of mind, that is fundamentally important. From this point of view the scholars who have seen the synoptic gospel summed up in the Sermon on the Mount cannot have been altogether wrong.

*   *   *

But see what a contrast to this we have in St. Paul. It is not that he denies the validity of this psychological approach. Far from it. The need for faith, for moral conduct, and for the expectation of judgment is all there. But something of a very different type is added to it. St. Paul is concerned not only with the psychology of salvation but also with what one might call its biology or, better, its ontology.

If psychology is concerned with the mind, biology is concerned with the life, and ontology with the actual being. St. Paul does not think the claims of Jesus are satisfied when our minds are directed towards him. We need, in an almost physical sense, to be 'in Christ.' Actually, as we know from our Prayer of Humble Access 'that we may evermore dwell in him and he in us,' the spatial metaphor has no particular significance. What is implied is that we should have so intimate a relation with Christ that it will no longer be a mere matter of our mind being drawn up alongside his, but that we may in a very real sense share his being.

To St. Paul essential Christianity was not just faith but incorporation into Christ. We must be grafted into Christ as a twig is grafted into a tree and grows into it so that the same sap, the same vitalizing force, flows through both. Or, to change the metaphor, we must be born again and become new creatures in Christ. In conjunction with him a new person is born in ourselves and grows in us from glory to glory until it reaches full maturity. Consequently every little duty we perform will be done in Christ.

*   *   *

The one evangelist who seems to have caught the full significance of this teaching and to have brought it out clearly in our Lord's own words is St. John. It is he who lays strong emphasis on the teaching that we must be born again, he who draws out the relation between the vine and its branches, he who in his wonderful sixth chapter insists that we must assimilate the two-fold nature of the God-made-man.

It is a teaching which we have never fully understood or acted upon. The return of St. Paul's day may remind us of it, and help us to realize with fresh intensity the great truth that the Christian life is essentially a living out of the Christ who is within.

THE CHRISTIAN CITIZEN

IT is never easy for us to realize the difficulties that faced our first forefathers in the faith. No sooner was the first fine ecstasy of their conversion over than they began to see in what a hard world they dwelt. Everything was new to them: how were they to adapt themselves to the changed conditions?

They had been born again: they had become citizens of the Kingdom of Heaven. But they were still members of a secular society, and that society no longer looked upon them with friendly eyes. Were they to return the dislike and put themselves into a permanent state of opposition, or were they to ignore it and as far as possible keep themselves from contact with both the Pagan and the Jewish worlds? They needed to think out their whole situation afresh.

In to-day's epistle St. Paul gives the Roman Christians a new philosophy of life; states his reasons for the attitude he advises; and ends by describing tersely the character of the good citizen.

The first thing they must remember is that government is an ordinance of God. Even though it may sometimes seem harsh and unjust, yet it is necessary in order to maintain law and order. Without it we should have anarchy and chaos, and that would be quite contrary to the will of God. It is therefore the Christian's duty as far as possible to support 'the powers that be.'

*   *   *

St. Paul gives four reasons for advising this attitude. First, it is the best way in which to keep on the right side of the law, and so pass one's time in peace and quiet. The very purpose of government is to ensure that the wheels of common life revolve smoothly and with the least possible inconvenience to the individual. If we wish to enjoy this benefit we must make our own contribution to the organization that makes it possible.

Second, we shall thus be able to escape the horrid sensation of fear. Government has no terror for the good man, but only for the evil-doer. In these days when detective novels and gangster films depict for us so vividly the constant terror in which a pursued man lives, we ought to find it easy to appreciate this point.

Third, this is the only way in which we can enjoy the fruits of our own expenditure. We pay taxes precisely in order to maintain government in being. How foolish and illogical it is to thwart our own ends by ignoring or actively disobeying the law. It is to waste our own money.

Fourth, above all we should be obedient to government for conscience's sake. If good order is in accordance with the will of God, then we shall surely suffer from a bad conscience when we transgress the law.

*   *   *

What then is the character of the Christian citizen? It is one to which a rebellious spirit is abhorrent. This is not always understood. To-day many people seem to regard it as a compliment to be described as a 'rebel.' There are indeed times when the Christian man finds himself compelled for conscience's sake to resist the powers that be, but he will do it with the grestest reluctance.

So far from manifesting a rebellious spirit the Christian citizen will be anxious to render to all and sundry the respect due to them. He will live in an atmosphere of continuous courtesy. It is not merely that he will not try to dodge income-tax and Customs duties or to 'fiddle' his expense account, but he will, whether as pedestrian or motorist, observe the rules of the road and spare other people as much trouble as possible.

Courtesy and respect must become part of the ingrained character of the Christian citizen. After all, we appreciate these virtues when shown to us by others; why should we not display them ourselves? They will help to keep us from the grosser forms of violation of the law. In any case, what are they but the expression of that *agape* or love which is the fundamental law of the Christian life?

CONVERSATION PIECE

Epiphany V   *Colossians* 3. 12

THE picture painted for us in to-day's epistle is that of a primitive, unsophisticated Christian community whose grasp of religion is fresh and firm, and in which the mysteries of God's redeeming love are talked about as freely and naturally as the weather.

No one who has never met such a community, and whose own religion has been bottled up by generations of shyness, reserve and self-restraint, will find it easy to understand or appreciate the picture St. Paul here draws as a 'conversation piece' of the early Church. Yet it is well worth studying.

The source of the new, bubbling excitement is found in the 'word of Christ.' That must mean surely the teaching which has been handed over to the infant community in the apostolic tradition. It is something fresh, exciting, powerful. Those who received it are full of it: it dwells in them richly: they cannot help talking about it.

That is good, says St. Paul, but do it with wisdom. All this talk must not be for novelty (in order to be in the fashion), nor for controversy (to beat others in argument); but in real, practical sagacity, with an eye to as much everyday usefulness as women's conversation about a new stitch in knitting or a new dish in cooking.

*   *   *

This kind of conversation will be marked by a great cheerfulness, and that cheerfulness will issue from time to time in song. To most people song is a natural expression of well-being. A casual collection of Welshmen on a beach, suddenly called upon to help man the windlass when the lifeboat is being drawn up on shore after a practice spin, fall naturally into the singing, with robust and splendid harmonies, of the nursery rhymes of their childhood.

To fourth-century Christians the chanting of the creed was as inspiring a song of triumph as was the Marseillaise to a later generation of Frenchmen. Augustine was stirred to profound emotion when, still a pagan, he heard in the great church at Milan the antiphonal singing of the psalms by Ambrose's congregation. Who can calculate how much the German Reformation owed to Luther's gift of song, or the Evangelical revival in England to the poetry and music of the Wesleys?

The power of music is almost universal. But there is one condition to its value in religion: it must be 'with grace in your hearts to the Lord.' There must be a free uplifting of our inner spirit in genuine praise of God.

*   *   *

This means that all we do must be under the inspiration of Christ. The spirit of our Christian conversation and the uplift of our Christian song must overflow the rest of our lives.

Our conversation in the outside world must reflect the spirit of the Christian community. That is not to say that it must be obviously pious, but it must be the echo of the word of Christ, dwelling in us richly in all wisdom. Where we are normally smart or boastful or just full of ourselves, we shall now be full of the spirit of Jesus.

So also all that we do will be an expression of our thanks to God in Christ. It will no longer be we who act but he who acts within us. His name, his character, will dominate our own until we shall be willingly and consciously spending our lives in helpfulness to others.

This means that the term 'conversation' as here used will cover not only our talk, but the conduct of our whole lives. That indeeed is its meaning as employed in the Authorized Version. 'Our conversation,' says St. Paul, 'is in heaven,' which means that heaven is our home-town, the place where we were born and brought up and where we acquired our accent and our code of manners. Of that upbringing we must never be ashamed, but most show it in its best light both in dialogue and in conduct. So by God's grace we may be able to restore something of its primitive freshness to the Christian community.

ABIDING IN CHRIST

Epiphany VI   1 *St. John* 3. 1

THE most striking phrase in to-day's epistle is 'abiding in Christ.'

What does it mean to abide in Christ? It is specially interesting to find out, both because of the possibilities the phrase contains and also because it is in effect the centre of St. John's theology. It is very unlike anything we should ourselves normally say: it is foreign to our natural mode of speech. We cannot expect it to be easy of explanation. It requires discussion on at least three levels.

First, we must try to understand it socially. To abide in Christ is to be a faithful member of the Christian community. St. Paul describes the Church as the Body of Christ and each member as a limb of that body. To abide in Christ must therefore mean to be so attached to the Church that its life becomes part of ours.

As we abide in this Body of Christ we are affected in every part of our being. It goes a long way towards moulding our manner of thought. It certainly affects our conduct. Above all it makes us new creatures in that we become beings whose main characteristic is that of worship. In this environment one habitually thinks of God and raises one's heart to him in adoration and praise. This is the very breath of life to the faithful Christian.

*   *   *

If we thus think first of this phrase in its social meaning, we must go on to interpret it in a psychological way. To abide in Christ is to have the mind of Christ. Paul exhorts us to 'put on Christ.' On this level to abide in him means to enter into his mind, to think his thoughts, to fulfil his intentions.

The good actor lives his part. He does not 'put on an act.' For the time being he *is* the character he represents. The preacher in the pulpit and the priest at the altar strive to forget themselves and to remember that they are parsons, *personae*, representatives of God and his Church. Only so can they be sure of speaking 'in character' and not disgracing the gospel they deliver. Even the quality of everyday friendship is decided by the extent to which we can in imagination and will sympathize, that is, share the same experiences, or suffer with, one another.

St. Augustine analysed the contents of human personality as affection, memory and will. If we are to abide psychologically in Christ, all these faculties must be engaged. We must love him with all our heart. We must constantly recall all we know about him—otherwise how can we ever hope to be like him? And above all our wills must be continually active to do what he commands and to follow his lead. The whole imaginative side of our being must be exercised in bringing him vividly before us.

*   *   *

To abide in Christ psychologically is immensely assisted by our abiding in him socially, that is, in his Church. But even so it would remain much more difficult if there were not a third way in which we may abide in him, that is, by participating in his actual being. Christ himself urged us to abide in him as he abides in us. And he compared this mutual indwelling to the way in which he and his Father share the same life. This is what we mean by abiding in Christ ontologically, that is, sharing the same being.

It is this that gives us the confidence that we may abide in Christ in both heart and mind. If we know that he has entered into our essential being, we may hope that he will show his presence there by enabling us to think, speak and act as he himself would do in our situation. If we are one with him as he and his Father are one, we must 'abide in him' both in the depth of our inmost being and also in our surface lives before the eyes of men.

St. Paul says he once knew a man 'in Christ.' The New English Bible translates his phrase, 'I knew a Christian man.' How wonderful it would be if every Christian man were truly a man who abides 'in Christ.' And how helpful it would be if Christ were truly the sphere in which Christian friends knew each other.

TIME OF PREPARATION

IN Lent we make a special effort to share with God in
his self-imposed task of redeeming his own creation.
Septuagesima not only reminds us how he made it in the
beginning and is re-making it to-day, but also introduces
a period of preparation during which we can decide
the lines of our own special effort.

There will be many who will be arranging their Lent
rule as eagerly as they will be planning their summer
holidays. In both cases it is good to have plenty of time
to think things over.

In arrangements such as these it is well not to attempt
too much. Our Lent rule should not be stiff or rigorous.
It should be well within our capacity. It is better to have
a time-table sparsely filled and to stick to it, rather than
to have one crowded with detail and to find ourselves
leaving half of it out.

Also, our rule should be positive rather than negative.
In the traditional trilogy, alms-giving, prayer and fasting,
self-denial or fasting occupies only a third of the space
and is placed last. Self-denial is a necessary part of Lent
observance, but it should look beyond itself to some positive
good. Pruning is not an end in itself: it is intended to
produce better flower and fruit.

*   *   *

The short-time purpose of the fast is to strengthen our
own character. Asceticism, from the Greek word *askesis*,
is simply training, a metaphor taken from the Olympic
games. St. Paul in the Epistle speaks of the shadow-boxing
which is part of the customary exercises before the pugilist

is fit to enter the ring. Only St. Paul warns us that the Christian's training is not a game: it is something that must be taken in deadly earnest.

Perhaps for this reason most of our forefathers in the faith preferred military metaphors. They were accustomed to a special measure of fasting every Wednesday and Friday. To these days they gave the name of Stations, from the Latin word for standing. It had a varied military significance and was sometimes used for a barracks, but here probably as the day on which the Christian soldiers made a special stand against the enemies of the soul. For the soldier 'to have a station' meant to be put on guard duty, and for the Christian it meant to hold a fast.

Of course we make jokes about the puny and even childish things we invent as the objects of our fasting or self-denial. But that does not matter so long as we do not make too much of them, but use them as means to an end. Dean Inge says somewhere that to deny ourselves in small things is the surest way to gain control of our whole nature.

*   *   *

But even this, commendable as it may be, is not the ultimate aim of the season for which we are now preparing. What we really want to do is to come nearer to Christ. What we desire is to acquire his mind, his way of looking at things. This we can only do by learning to know him better and to love him more.

That is why we must provide some place in our rule for special reading. Nowadays several Lent books are published every year to tell us more about God and his ways. Our mind needs to be enlightened and our knowledge enlarged.

But we have to know Jesus not only intellectually but sympathetically. That is why we shall need some extra time for worship; so that we can spend longer in his presence and commune with him more freely. We cannot really get to know another person unless we spend a good deal of time in his company.

And finally, of course, we have to know him practically, so that we shall instinctively do the things he would do. It is only when you have begun to *think* in another language that you can talk it at all fluently. It is not until we have the mind of Christ that we can naturally and habitually perform the acts of Christ.

It is worth while then using this time of preparation well. There is a great deal to plan and to do.

OUR WEAKNESS

THE Church is the home of peace and love: its members live in constant accord with each other and with God. So we have been taught, and so we know it ought to be.

In actual experience we learn differently. This description applies to an ideal Church which has no obvious existence. The Church we really know does not seem to differ in this respect from other human societies. Its members are often at feud with each other; they show the same pettiness as members of secular organizations; they share the same ambitions and the same impatience.

This discovery is always disconcerting, especially to the recent convert. In the height of newly aroused enthusiasm we expect everything to be perfect. We forget that the Church on earth is composed of human beings with the same failings and weaknesses as others. They may be on their way to perfection, but they are certainly not perfected as yet.

Then perhaps we begin to look back to see if things have always been like this. Was there never a time when Christians lived together in complete harmony? Can we not put our finger on any one spot and say 'There was the Church precisely as it should be?' St. Paul's Epistles and the Acts of the Apostles answer, 'No.' This is one of the tragedies of our earthly existence.

*   *   *

St. Paul had in this respect some bad experiences. His worst was at Corinth. There the party spirit had threatened to break up the Christian community into sections. Added

46

to this there had been a moral lapse in which Paul's own judgment had been defied. Things had got so bad that his authority had been repudiated. Rather than exacerbate feelings further, he had been obliged to leave. To-day's epistle shows us his efforts to defend himself.

He does so on three grounds. First he accuses the Corinthians of rank folly in mistaking the motives of his opponents. They will let these men domineer over them, tie them up with unnecessary regulations, and even take their money. In contrast he calls in witness his own undoubted status as a member by birth and training of the most select circle of the Jews and also by appointment as a messenger of Christ.

Then he enumerates his labours and sufferings on behalf of the gospel. It is a terrible list: it should have convinced any fair-minded enquirer of his good faith. Who could possibly have endured all this if he had not been wholehearted in his belief and service of Christ?

And thirdly he points to the actual work he has already done in his ministry, the constant care he has taken in administering the affairs of the local churches, the sympathy and love he has shown for every individual Christian who has come in contact with him; all these things are well known and should have given conclusive proof of his sincerity and authority.

*   *   *

St. Paul hates himself for saying all this. It has been wrung out of him by the sheer necessity of the situation. In the end he knows that no such argument can be conclusive. All that he can do is to acknowledge his own weakness and insufficiency. He throws himself on the mercy of God and asks his people to understand.

Perhaps he realizes that he, too, may have been a little domineering. In any case boasting, however justified, will not do. But people who will not yield to self-assertion may be won over by an acknowledgment of incapacity. And Paul himself, when he admits his own want of self-confidence, may find a new confidence in God.

It is no doubt because of this psychological revelation that the epistle is set for our reading as we prepare for Lent. That season is not intended to build up our sense of superiority, but to make us recognize our weakness.

When we are weak, then, like St. Paul, we are strong. When we are emptied of ourselves, then there is room for God. When we are ready truly to stand on the same level with others, then we begin to arouse and to extend a common sympathy and mutual regard. In this way we may learn truly to be the Church.

THE GREATER VIRTUE

LOVE, it is generally agreed by Christian moralists, is
the greatest of the virtues, the foundation and guide
of all the rest. St. Paul in his 'ode to love' gives us a
poetic analysis of it. He describes first its necessity, then
its character, and finally its permanence.

First its necessity. The reason why we cannot do without it is that unless they are inspired by love all other
qualities lose their intrinsic value. Even a good deed
can be spoilt by being done from the wrong motive.
So love must be the ground of every virtue.

Paul enumerates specific details. I may speak with the
most attractive eloquence; I may have the keenest insight
into men and affairs; I may have the kind of inner drive
that moves mountains of difficulty; I may even be so
devoted to the cause I serve that I am prepared sacrifice
my life for it. Yet, if these fine qualities are not inspired
by a real desire to do the best I possibly can for my fellow-
men, they are really wasted.

Everyone is familiar with the phrase 'as cold as charity.'
That means that even our alms-giving can be so denuded
of all real sympathy for the person we deign to help that it
can repel the beneficiary like an insult.

*   *   *

That introduces the second division of St. Paul's hymn,
in which he discloses the character of true love. Again he
does it, not by way of a general description, but by giving
illustrative details.

First, he says, love is characterized by its essential
kindness and patience. We had an instance of that the

other evening on television when an ex-prison warder
was saying how many of his former charges had responded
to proper treatment, had made good on discharge, and
still maintained a friendly correspondence with him
years after their term had been completed.

Then love, says St. Paul, is characterized by a complete
absence of any thought of self. It is never selfish or boastful; it is never blatant or bumptious; it never puts self
first.

Again it is always prepared to face the truth, and indeed
seeks it out. It is never malicious or spiteful, and would
never stoop to slander. Nor would it out of envy or
jealousy relapse into any kind of sulkiness that makes
impossible the resumption of good relations.

Further, love is characterized by its determination
never to give up. It is without limit. Mere sentimentalism,
which is sometimes taken weakly for a kind of love, is
shallow and easily dispensable. It marks no more solid
emotion than the facile tear at the theatre or in the cinema.
Real love is so strong that it infuses its stability into other
virtues like faith, and hope, and endurance.

*   *   *

The fact is that love, true love, has the quality of permanence. All else, including its own counterfeits, may be
partial and spasmodic. But true love persists. In its
earnest set of the will it has about it an adult quality
that inspires confidence. Many other excellent qualities
are ephemeral. Your most exquisite ecstasy lasts but a
moment, the finest sermon comes to an end, even knowledge has a way of disappearing, but love is stable and
enduring.

We have only to look back to our childhood to see how
everything has always been on the move: all has been
growth and change. But now it is the very pride of our

manhood that we have reached maturity. That does not mean that there is no further growth. We look forward, now that the lines of our development are settled, to the dawning of an ultimate perfection. In love then let us be our age, steadfast in our determination to serve the highest interests of every individual with whom we come in contact.

Such love will give new life and vigour to faith and hope. They, too, in spite of what the hymn says, may achieve a kind of immortality. But love, their basis and inspiration, is the greatest of them all.

HOLINESS THE AIM

IT is extraordinary how much St. Paul can pack into a short passage. In to-day's epistle he is exhorting his readers to strive after the highest possible standard of Christian living.

In a few verses he shows how this ideal may be achieved in three different ways; one which is the way of renunciation, another which is the way of affirmation, and the third which is a combination of the two and therefore paradoxical.

The first is the way of renunciation, an aspect of the Christian life much in our minds during Lent. Paul gives his own experiences as an example; and shows how he has tried to establish his position as God's minister 'although the effort has involved much suffering, affliction, trouble, sorrow, even beating and imprisonment. I have been mobbed and I have been grossly overworked with my strength reduced by sleeplessness and lack of food.'

All this Paul had deliberately chosen for himself when he threw up his position as a rising leader of his nation and joined the humiliated servants of Christ.

It is this spirit that we try to acquire in Lent. Our little acts of self-denial, grotesquely small as they are, are intended to remind us that we do not truly belong to this world at all. We have been bought with a price; our lives are hid with Christ in God. We have torn our real ambitions away from this life, except in so far as it provides opportunity for our absorbing passion to do the will of God.

*   *   *

This proviso shows that there is an affirmative aspect of our life here. We have renounced this world in order to affirm the claims of the other, unseen, world with its entirely different set of values. St. Paul is not ashamed to say what he strove after:

'I have not failed in innocence, knowledge, patience, kindness, inspiration of the Holy Spirit, sincerity of love, truth in argument or power of God. I have dealt doughty blows for righteousness to right and left, and have remained indifferent to glory and shame, to renown and disrepute.'

One is reminded how great a part has been played by the desire for holiness in all the great religious movements.

Athanasius in the fourth century was not fighting for the strict letter of orthodoxy so much as for the freedom of the Christian to be incorporated into Christ who is perfect God and perfect man. Luther and Calvin brought about the explosion of the Reformation in order to clear away the mediæval debris which, they believed, was impeding that particular process. Wesley formed his original 'holy club' to help undergraduates to advance towards moral and spiritual perfection in Christ. Of Keble, Pusey and Newman it would be difficult to say which was most completely absorbed in the pursuit of sheer goodness as taught by Christ.

*   *   *

Mere self-denial then is not enough: there must also be the active striving after the best and highest. If the Christian's life is marked by a constant 'No' to the world, the flesh and the devil, it is also marked by a constant 'Yes' to all that is true and lovely and of good repute. This mingled yes and no is what gives its apparently paradoxical appearance to the Christian's attitude to the world.

St. Paul is not afraid of the apparent contradiction. He takes each charge made against him and sets its opposite truth side by side with it. 'I am an impostor and yet genuine, unknown and yet openly approved, dead and yet very much alive, beaten but not killed, gloomy yet always cheerful, poor yet bringing riches to many, penniless yet possessing everything.'

This is not just playing with words, or logic-chopping. The paradox is resolved in actual experience. Even where they seem most contradictory the epithets are found to be true in the everyday living of the Christian life. If we gladly accept death to the world, we find a glorious new life open to the spirit.

THE WILL OF GOD

COUNTLESS men, women and children through all the ages have been anxious to do the will of God. Before they could do it, they have had to have some idea of what it is.

The more enlightened have realized that there must be a distinct will for each person. And many have lived to realize the mistakes they have made with regard to their own affairs. But, apart from the specific purpose for each individual, there must be a general will of God for the whole human race, a plan with which God has made us and planted us in this material world. What is the will of God for mankind as a whole?

St. Paul at least has no doubt on the matter. In the epistle he tells us quite clearly and succinctly: 'This is the will of God, even your sanctification.'

How did St. Paul know? He had been taught it all his life. The man who as a student sat at the feet of Gamaliel had imbibed it as part of the necessary erudition of his childhood. It was what the sacred scriptures of his people were all about. The history of the Jews was the story of God's education of his people for this purpose. Through the law and the prophets God led them in the way of sanctification in order that they might in their turn sanctify others.

This was one lesson that Paul did not have to unlearn when he became a Christian. The Jesus who appeared to him on the road to Damascus and secured his allegiance was equally insistent on the need for sanctification.

*   *   *

But what does sanctification mean? It means 'making holy.' That is what is demanded of all the children of God. 'Be ye holy even as I am holy.' And being holy means being good in the highest degree. That is why man would have needed sanctification even if he had not sinned. He would have needed a steady growth in goodness until he reached the perfection to which he was called.

It is true that there is another sense to sanctification. It also means being set apart, dedicated to the service of God. But, since God is himself holy, to be dedicated to his service means being holy also in the ethical sense.

For that reason we find St. Paul speaking sometimes of sanctification as something already given, communicated to Christians at baptism. 'Ye were washed, ye were sanctified, ye were justified in the name of the Lord Jesus Christ.' Sometimes, however, he speaks of it as still to be accomplished or at least completed: 'Having therefore these promises, beloved, let us cleanse ourselves from all defilement of flesh and spirit, perfecting holiness in the fear of God.'

St. Paul sees this sanctification as something interior to the spirit of man, a character that is bestowed upon him when he is first set apart for the service of God, and that grows and develops as he exercises it in all godliness of living.

*   *   *

Here then we see the purpose of our Lenten observance. This is not a period of austerity for austerity's sake. It is not a kind of spiritual masochism, deliberately inflicting wounds upon itself. It is an attempt to bring to the forefront of our lives the purpose for which we are actually living. It is the genuine asceticism, the training of the Christian athlete who, although he always tries to keep fit as a matter of course, nevertheless recognizes that he needs periods of special effort to make him capable of the great trials of strength from time to time demanded of him.

Nor is the sanctification, the holiness 'without which no man shall see the Lord,' something outside ourselves which we must be for ever reaching out to grasp, but a grace already bestowed upon us which we must allow to show itself and practise in the outer world. If it is true that what is really harmful can come only from within, it must be also true that what is really good must also come from within, where it has been already planted by God. True sanctification is nothing less than the life of Christ nourished within the soul.

WALK IN LIGHT

'BE ye followers of God and walk in love.' There in a
nutshell is contained the Christian gospel. Almost
complete, but not quite; for it also needs the statement
of our reconciliation with God through Christ and his
continuous power that upholds us during the period of
our sanctification.

Nevertheless, as it stands it gives us our directions for
the way. God goes before us, as he did for the children
of Israel in the wilderness, a great and a shining light.
We who follow are bathed in that light. It is the light of
love, shining into our hearts and reflected from them as
from a mirror, radiating back to God, our leader, and out
to our companions on the way. We walk in love.

It is not often that the Bible bids us follow the example
of Christ—it seems almost to shrink from setting us too high
a task—but here it does, giving us the encouragement of
knowing that he has trodden this way before us. We are
to give ourselves up entirely to the following of God, as
Christ did before us, making of himself a whole burnt-
offering so perfect and complete that it fulfilled and
ended the long line of Jewish sacrifices which had been
offered to God down the ages since the first calling of his
people.

*   *   *

But, however light it is ahead of us, the epistle leaves us
in no doubt that it is dark all around. In that darkness
lurk the enemies of the soul. Paul has no hesitation in
defining them.

He sees the chief enemy of the soul in the sexuality of the pagan society in which his converts lived. It was difficult for them not to come in contact with it for it pervaded literature, conversation, the arts, business, even religion itself. They must see it clearly for what it was, and not besmirch the God-given life of the body by descending into licentiousness of thought, word or deed.

It seems that there are recurrent periods in the history of mankind when this particular enemy acquires a special persistence. There can be little doubt that we are going through such a period at the present time. It is therefore supremely important for us to be on our guard against it both in ourselves and in society. We must do what we can to assist the forces that are even now gathering to cleanse this corruption from our public life. This we can do, not merely by negative resistance but by positive endeavours to provide for others and for ourselves occupation for mind and body which is good and wholesome. This is the true 'giving of thanks' which should characterize the Christian—the grateful employment of both work and leisure for the greater appreciation of God's good gifts to mankind.

*   *   *

St. Paul emphasizes the lesson by reverting to the figure of light. The Christian's life is an active one of peace, love and joy. So far from dehumanizing the individual or the society in which he lives, the Christian brings to it a fresh access of gladness in the appreciation of its vast possibilities.

The Christian has actually partaken of the very nature of that light that proceeds from God and illumines his way. 'Ye were sometimes darkness, but now are ye light in the Lord.' We are to be what by grace we already are in potentiality. When we were baptized we were brought

E

out of darkness into light, and the light has ever since been with us. We are now intended to be the lights of the world, kindled by him who is already the one Light of the World. We are incandescent with his flame. We must give light, not by forced, uneasy striving, but by being what we are.

We all know how much better house and garden, city and church, look on a bright day. The light brings a lift of the heart and a new beauty to a familiar scene. It also reveals what is ugly: but it makes us feel that even the bad spots may be reformed when we clearly recognize them for what they are.

THE ASSEMBLY OF THE FIRST-BORN

IT is to be hoped that in churches where there is more than one Eucharist on a Sunday the congregation will be given the chance at least once of hearing the alternative epistle (*Heb.* 12. 22–24). It is one of the most uplifting panegyrics on the Church to be found in scripture. Its ringing phrases overleap the bounds of logical order, but by that very fact induce in the reader a feeling of the intense excitement obviously felt by the writer.

To analyse an emotional appeal is almost impossible. Yet, if we take the risk and try to dissect the passage, we can discern a certain arrangement of thought. It is easiest to start in the middle. There one finds the central thought of the Church as it exists on earth. That central thought is approached by a preliminary picture of the Church in heaven, and it is succeeded by a concluding description of God the universal Ruler seated on the throne of judgment.

*   *   *

To begin with the central thought: the Church on earth is described as the general assembly of the first-born, whose names are written in heaven. This is to picture heaven under the social guise of a city. In any city of the ancient world the general assembly was the body of citizens gathered together for a common purpose. There would be a 'voters' register' on which would be duly recorded the names of all full members of the city. In God's case the register is carefully kept in heaven itself. Every name on it is there because the person so designated has been called out and chosen individually by God himself.

Further, those whose names are thus written in what the Apocalypse calls the Lamb's book of life are described as the first-born. That means that they are the original nucleus of what is destined to become the universal Church. The term 'first-born' also carries with it the overtone of special affection. 'This is my beloved Son.' The citizens duly enrolled in God's kingdom are privileged to share the affection God bestows upon the Son in whom he is well pleased.

*　　　*　　　*

This picture of the 'little flock' here upon earth is preceded by a glimpse of the Church as it exists eternally. It is the centre of the infinite universe, the temple-crowned mountain, the holy city, the place of pilgrimage for all God's people now translated into the infinite sphere, inhabited by an innumerable company of angels.

The term 'company' is an interesting word, implying a gathering for a great festal occasion. There is joy in heaven. Whatever great plans may be carried out there, all is done in an atmosphere of continual bliss. We remember how often Jesus in his parables had depicted the Kingdom of Heaven as a feast. Here that spirit of supreme content is pictured as the state in which the angels always dwell. It is the self-same atmosphere that is characteristic of the Church on earth, at least in its ideal form. To have such a picture before their eyes must surely have been a constant inspiration to those who had just emerged from a quarrelsome and dangerous world.

*　　　*　　　*

The final section carries us, after our glimpse of the Church on earth, into heaven again. Here the emphasis is on the figure seated upon the throne of the universe, God the judge of all, as he is so often depicted both in the works of theologians and in the creations of the great artists, ruling supreme out of eternity over the events of time.

And there too is Jesus, the agent of this new phase in the story of redemption, who by his Incarnation forms the link between the earthly and the heavenly Jerusalem. It was his Spirit who in the past had perfected the life of the just men as he is now perfecting the character of the present members of the Church on earth. All, whether on earth or in heaven, are knit together by that Spirit in one eternal home of love and joy and peace. That is what the Church, the mother of the first-born, really means.

OUR HIGH PRIEST

Lent V   *Hebrews* 9. 11

TO the outsider the Epistle to the Hebrews must seem
an oddly mysterious book. But to the Christian,
brought up to understand the stories of the Old Testament,
it is also a fascinating exposition of God's ways with man
through the ages.

The author does not take up the position maintained
by some later Christian writers, that the Jews never did
manage to understand their own law, He gives it the
traditional interpretation, but then proceeds to show
how in almost every detail it had its echo in the life of
Christ. This he does by explaining that the various
elements in the old ceremonial regulations were symbols
of the work and character of Jesus, who thus fulfilled and
brought to an end the Jewish law.

An example is to be seen in the office of the High Priest.
He was indeed a great person in his own right, but he
was only a kind of shadow of the Christ who was to come.
So with all the old customs. They were valid enough for a
period. But they had been intended as indications that
something greater and more substantial was to arrive.

Perfection was reached in the new dispensation.
There was a new High Priest, a new Tabernacle, a new
Sacrifice. These were not just for a time, they were, and
were intended to be, eternal.

*   *   *

So the author launches his great emotive appeal to his
readers. He wishes to draw out all the love the Jewish
people had for their law and to direct it towards Christ.

Christ had not destroyed the law, but fulfilled it in his own person. He was the true, the perfect High Priest. The anti-type for which the type had been made.

From this appeal to the emotions the writer moves to the sphere of logic. Of course the old sacrifices, offered by the High Priest, had a certain efficacy. They removed taboos and enabled the holiness of God and the sinfulness of man to be recognized. On that basis they encouraged divine worship to proceed.

Everyone must acknowledge, however, that these remedies did not provide a permanent cure for human ills, otherwise they would not have had to be so frequently repeated. But, if the offering of mere beasts and birds could have such an effect, however limited, it must be obvious that Christ's voluntary self-sacrifice, the perfect High Priest offering himself willingly for his people, must have a universal and perfect efficacy.

Whatever they thought of the logic, people who accepted Christ's offering on their behalf did find themselves caught up into that sphere of eternal significance in which his sacrifice operated. It was like being born all over again. They had a direct access to the eternal God and they were filled with a new life.

*   *   *

Finally the writer moves from the typological and logical levels to the moral. All this fulfilment of the old law and this endowment of believers with a new life was meant to have its effect in the daily conduct of Christian people. Because his old sinful life had been atoned for in Christ and he had made a fresh start, the Christian had entered into a new covenant with God; he had been put into a new relationship with the Father. And this relationship must issue in a different code of conduct.

Here was realized God's age-long promise to his people. This was no temporary arrangement, no partial restoration of a vanished Eden. This was the granting of an eternal inheritance. Those who entered into this new agreement with God were the truly called, the real Israel, manifesting in their daily lives their lasting fellowship with God.

We of this generation are members of this goodly company. We have already entered upon our inheritance. We have to see that our lives reflect the glory that has been revealed to us. What is Lent for, but to help us recognize our privileges more clearly and to live up to them more thoroughly?

HYMN ON THE INCARNATION

Palm Sunday   *Philippians* 2. 5

PALM SUNDAY'S epistle is one of the most famous passages from St. Paul's letters.

It consists of an early Christian hymn on the Incarnation. It must often have been used in church services before Paul memorized it and quoted it when writing to the Philippians. Indeed it is probably the earliest description of the Incarnation to be found in Christian, or any other, literature. Its closest companion is the somewhat similar hymn that forms the prologue to the Fourth Gospel.

It begins with the picture of the Christ as he was for all eternity—in the form of God, that is in the same order of existence, the same quality of being as God. Yet, although he was of the highest grade of essential being, he did not think that equality with God was a prize to be grasped and clutched. When he considered the needs of men he was willing voluntarily for their sake to surrender it.

The thought of the highest becoming the lowest is central to Christianity. The Maundy Thursday commemoration of the feet-washing, when the Saviour of the World performed the function of a slave, still keeps before our minds its importance in a symbol. When the Sovereign distributes her Maundy money we may think there is no necessity for that kind of thing in a Welfare State, but it is good that we should be constantly reminded of the divine humility and try to imitate it in our own lives.

*   *   *

This initial surrender of the eternal Christ was made effective upon earth in two stages. He first 'emptied himself' of his divine prerogatives. The effect of becoming man was that he could not within his activity as man exercise such supernatural powers as omniscience and omnipotence.

Some teachers have concluded from this effect that the eternal Word of God laid aside his divinity—emptied himself in an almost literal sense of his essential character as divine and became merely a man among men. But this is to mistake the effect for the method. It would also make it difficult for us to see how he could in that way reveal the divinity he had laid aside.

It is better not to press the metaphor too far, but to think of the Word expressing himself as completely as possible through human nature. The Incarnation was a translation of divinity into the terms of humanity. The true nature of Godhead could be judged through the humility of Christ.

The second stage in this peculiar kind of self-emptying was when, having become man, the Word humbled himself still further to become the lowest kind of man there was—a condemned criminal dying on the cross. It was not sufficient just to become man; he must become what in the common estimate was the meanest type of man. Only so could he plumb the depths of human nature and redeem it completely from the bottom to the top.

It is such self-sacrifice that, even in our generation, missionaries and priest-workers have tried to imitate in their own lives. We can copy it too in some degree if we refuse to let privilege and pride of place stand between us and the lowliest of our fellow-men.

*   *   *

This humiliation is by no means the end of the story. It is the prelude to a glorious exaltation—the bestowal of a name above every name. As emperor is above king, so Jesus will be exalted above every earthly honour, because his dominion will be universal. His title to authority will include the whole universe of men and things. St. Paul's thought is echoed by St. John: the greatest glory must be ushered in by the severest humiliation. 'I, *if I be lifted up*, will draw all men unto me.'

It is an easy lesson, hard to learn. We must not be cast down by sufferings, failures, manifest weakness, and imperfection all around us. The way to heaven lies under the cross. We must learn to take what is coming to us, not merely resigning ourselves to an unpleasant necessity but confident that by it a door will be opened into the glory in which our forerunner already reigns.

RISEN WITH CHRIST

TO-DAY'S epistle give us a whole doctrine of Easter
in a nutshell. It speaks of the new life we share
with the risen Christ, of the future glory in which it will
issue, and of the change in character and moral conduct
that it immediately demands.

The first thing we have to remember is that life is
completely new for those who are in Christ. This is not
easy, because we ourselves have been 'in Christ' almost
from the time of our natural birth. We have really known
no other life: how then are we to distinguish its new-
ness?

We must think what life would be like without Christ.
We must remember how dreadful we ourselves feel in our
worst moments. We must try to imagine the immense
revolution in the lives of those who have turned from
darkness to light, whether as converted heathen in
missionary lands or converted profligates in a Christian
country.

It is from that kind of condition, which still remains
just round the corner, that we have been exempted.
'There but for the grace of God go I.' The life that we
actually live is hid with Christ in God. 'If ye then be
risen with Christ, seek those things that are above.'

*   *   *

Then in one swift sentence we are reminded of the
ultimate issue of this Christ-life into the splendour of
heaven. 'When Christ, who is our life, shall appear, then
shall ye also appear with him in glory.'

The future re-appearance of Christ is assumed as certain. One does not have to argue about it or try to prove it. It is seen as the natural consequence of his Resurrection. After the tomb was emptied he was no longer tied to earth by a physical body. He could come and go as he pleased. He was at home in two environments as diving birds are at home in the water or in the air. It was natural therefore to expect his coming. And so he did come, in answer to their prayers, when they broke the Eucharistic bread together, in the constant influence of his Holy Spirit.

But one day he would come visibly in all the glory of the heaven that was now his normal dwelling. That would be a final appearance to change the constitution of the universe, when the time of probation would be over and all things would assume their everlasting condition.

In that day those who were in Christ would come with him. How could it be otherwise? They would share his triumph and lead those still alive on the earth into his everlasting joy.

*   *   *

To contemplate such a possibility, which is indeed a certainty for these who are 'risen with Christ,' is both exciting and encouraging. But the contemplation is not intended as an end in itself. It is meant to help us match our conduct to our hopes.

The Christian, if he has his head in heaven, still has his feet firmly planted on the ground. His may be the glory hereafter, but at the moment he has his life to live on the earth. The life of the risen Christ, which is one day to manifest itself in such ineffable glory, must now show its power and its beauty in every thought and word and action.

We must make it clear that we really are dead to the un-Christian manner of living. The deeds of darkness should be quite out of the question for us. The winter of our discontent must be truly excluded, and we must manifest a really vivid happiness in the ever-renewed life of Christ.

THE VICTORY OF FAITH

Easter I   1 *St. John* 5. 4

ST. JOHN, even more than most Christians of his
generation, lived in the spirit of the Resurrection. He
knew that what had happened on that Easter morning had
changed the whole situation of the world and of man
within it. He realized to the full the victory this implied
over all the pain and evil, the weakness and frustration
of the universe.

He realized also that before any man could call that
victory his own he must have some mental attitude, some
feeling, some instinct by which he could grasp it and make
it part of his own being. That attitude he called faith.
It is easy therefore to see how important it is that individual
Christians for their part should understand what this
faculty called faith really implies.

Faith is first of all, and most simply, acceptance. It is
acquiescence in the truth presented to us. When we
were children we were offered by our parents, by our
teachers, by the human environment in which we lived, a
certain attitude towards the world. We accepted it and
lived in it almost without thinking. But this simple
acceptance was sufficient to rule our conduct, dictate our
habits, and affect our characters. Later in life we find
this whole view challenged, and then we begin to see
that mere acceptance is not enough.

*   *   *

What we need now is something stronger than acceptance: we need a new attitude that can withstand the
challenge of an antagonistic world. It must be more

than a passive reception of the truth; it must be a firm, strong conviction that will impel us to action even if it involves defiance of the opposition. A child learning to swim is instructed in the right movements of his limbs on dry land, and he accepts this as he does his other lessons. But, when he is thrown into the water, unless he has some other instinct that will impel him to put his lesson into practice, he will drown.

Experience strengthens conviction. We are not asked to believe without evidence. No doubt the child has seen other swimmers, and so is encouraged to make his own attempts. Deuteronomy says that one witness is not enough. 'At the mouth of two, or three, witnesses shall a matter be established.' And so St. John says there are three witnesses to the manhood of Christ, and so to his Resurrection: the Spirit who proclaimed him, the water (his baptism) and the blood (his crucifixion).

We for our part also find evidence—the Bible, the Church, the sacraments, the lives of saintly people. Without some reasonable evidence faith may become mere superstition. But with it the whole man, intellect, affection, will, is justified in confirming the original acceptance and so reaching conviction.

*　　*　　*

Conviction, however, may be for a moment. Few of us can escape doubts of one kind or another. It would probably be a bad thing if we could, for then faith would not be tested or strengthened. A friend, we are told, is born for adversity. And faith, which is born as acceptance and continues as conviction, must grow into maturity as trust or loyalty.

It is in this respect that faith differs from knowledge. We sometimes think of knowledge as a higher kind of certitude. And so, in a sense, it is. But knowledge contains no moral element. We are not better or worse for knowing a thing or even a person. But to be capable of trust or loyalty we must be moral beings.

It is this final attitude of mind, this unshakeable trust ('Though he slay me, yet will I put my trust in him') that characterizes the true Christian. It is this that brings the power of the Resurrection into our inner lives, that translates it from being a matter of history into being a part of ourselves. It is this that gives us a share in the glory of Christ's Resurrection even here and now. This is the victory that overcometh the world, even our faith.

F

INJUSTICE SURMOUNTED

Easter II   1 *St. Peter* 2. 19

IT is somewhat unusual in the epistles to find a practical
lesson inculcated first, and then the theological reasons
on which it is based outlined afterwards. Normally we
get the doctrine first and the application later.

To-day's epistle follows the less usual order, and with
great effect. It may be that the latter part is really an
early Christian hymn. In which case the writer would be
quoting it to clinch his point, much as a modern preacher
will use some lines of poetry in his sermon. In any case
the lesson is stated stark and clear: 'It is a specially fine
thing if a man is prepared, because he has God in his
heart, to accept punishment without repining even when
he does not deserve it.' The word 'charis,' translated
'thankworthy,' is the word used elsewhere for grace,
favour, or free gift. It implies here something over and
above what you would expect in the ordinary line of
duty.

The advice is addressed to slaves and other lowly
members of the Christian Church exposed to the threat of
persecution. It is particularly important that they should
earn the good-will of their masters. They must show
that Christians are good members of the household and of
the state. Their Christian grace and fortitude should
stand them in good stead. Even if they would not be
prepared to put up with injustice for their own sake, they
must learn to do so for the sake of God and the brethren.

*   *   *

It must be remembered that the willingness to support
injustice without complaint is a special vocation for the

Christian. If one doubts it, there is always the example of Christ. And here we have one of the comparatively rare passages of scripture in which we are invited to take Jesus as our model and follow in his steps. He is not only our inspiration, or the source of our power; he is also our pattern by which we must rule our conduct.

Probably St. Peter is here calling to mind the events on Calvary. There, as Jesus hung upon the cross, silent and uncomplaining, one of the bandits being executed with him tried to find relief from the extremity of his own suffering by reviling the Figure that hung so quiet beside him. Jesus offered no answer to those insults but contented himself with ministering to the other thief who, even on the cross, sought comfort from him.

There are many difficult situations in everyday life in which we should be helped if we could ask ourselves the simple question: what in these circumstances would Jesus do? If we can find a sufficiently clear answer to that question, it is comparatively easy to go on to ask: what then would he have me do?

*   *   *

So we are given a lesson to learn and an example to copy. Finally we are given the theological reason on which both can be supported. In the crucifixion Christ was himself the supreme instance of suffering undeservedly inflicted. The sins he took with him to the cross were not his but ours. By his death he wiped them out. We, who have been joined to him, died to sin with him. Henceforth we live to righteousness, to the same kind of righteousness he showed, which includes the willingness to suffer on behalf of others.

It is a reflection of the great picture of the Suffering Servant in Isaiah 53. By his stripes we are healed. It may be that, if we are prepared to use this extra grace of undeserved suffering, some other may find relief because of what we do.

This was the more possible for the people to whom St. Peter wrote, and should be the more possible for us, because neither we nor they have been left alone. We have been brought into the close communion and fellowship of all the saints in the Church of God, for whom God himself is both Shepherd and Bishop. Under his care and protection and in their company we can attain to heights we never could have reached alone.

DIVERSE SITUATIONS

Easter III   1 *St. Peter* 2. 11

THE ambiguity that shrouds the origin of many early
documents will often lead rival historians to place
the same writing in widely different contexts. Few can
have experienced this fate in a more picturesque fashion
than the short scripture we know as 1 Peter.

At the moment, leaving out a number of subsidiary
suggestions, there are two main theories: one puts it in the
midst of the Neronian persecution, the other regards it as
part of the liturgy of Easter Eve. It would be difficult to
imagine two more sharply contrasted backgrounds. Yet
it is interesting to notice how the same moral and spiritual
lessons fit them both. It is that very similarity that
makes it hard for some scholars to choose between the two
situations.

*   *   *

If the first and more traditional view is correct, the
epistle was written at the moment when, after the burning
of Rome, Nero had accused the Christians of arson and
had begun his attempt to exterminate them. There was
every possibility that the persecution would spread to
Asia; and St. Peter on the eve of his own martyrdom
writes to encourage the Christians there and advise them
about their conduct.

They are to do their utmost to avoid arousing suspicion.
They must take care that none of them breaks any law
that will bring him into court. They must certainly
not attract attention or challenge punishment out of sheer
bravado. Yet if anyone is called upon to suffer 'for the
Name,' that is, on the sole charge of being a Christian,

79

then he must regard his opportunity so to serve the Master as the highest honour; and he must not fail either in straightforwardness or in courage.

From this point of view the epistle is a most valuable guide to the conduct proper for the Christian in face of opposition. He is to display at once the qualities of gentleness and strength, and he is in all things to follow the example of his Master who, 'when he was reviled, reviled not again, but committed himself to him that judgeth righteously.'

*　　　*　　　*

On the second view, the epistle really consists of a series of short homilies addressed to the catechumens during the long night vigil of the great service of Christian initiation, comprising baptism, confirmation, and first Communion. It is even suggested by Professor Cross (1 *Peter, a Paschal Liturgy*) that one can, by the exercise of a little imagination, fit the various sections of the document into the appropriate parts of the service.

In this case the warfare envisaged by the speaker is not a strife with the Roman government but against 'the world, the flesh and the devil.' The advice given is not addressed to people who feel the executioner's sword at their neck but to those who will have continually to deal with the trials and temptations to which all mankind is heir. No doubt these universal troubles would be exacerbated in the case of the catechumens by the fact that they would be living in the midst of suspicious and disapproving neighbours. But many in more peaceful times have had to do that.

*　　　*　　　*

Whether, then, in this document we have to deal with war-time 'orders of the day' or with a pastoral letter (showing incidentally how a bishop can allow his sermons to invade his correspondence), the lesson is much the same. It is the same, too, for Christians to-day, whether they live in Moscow or Mayfair. We are risen with Christ, and we must face every situation in the power of his Resurrection.

That means that we shall let Christ live out his life in us in all its courage, courtesy and love. If we are called upon to suffer with him, we shall take it patiently, adding our quota to the sum-total of the sufferings he endured for us. This we shall do in the assurance that, as by his stripes we are healed, so by his rising again we have become inheritors with him of life everlasting.

NO VARIABLENESS

Easter IV   *St. James* 1. 17

THERE is no experience so terrible, we are told, as
that of an earthquake. The reason for the terror is
that the very foundations of one's being seem to have been
dissolved. There is nothing steady or stable. The earth
rocks, the houses fall, the trees are torn up, the heavens
whirl, the very ground under your feet heaves and shakes.
There is no steadiness or support anywhere.

When you think of God, says St. James, you must think
of the very opposite of all that. He is steady, reliable,
always there, immutable, without any variation. He is
like a constant stream of light, before which all shifting
and changing shadows are banished, leaving one steadfast,
unchanging glow. He is indeed the Father of all the lights,
the source from which the heavenly bodies themselves
derive their illumination.

One might have feared some monotony from such a
description, but we are saved from that apprehension
because this light that streams so steadily upon the world
is all benevolence. It brings nothing but good. It meets
with its unfailing readiness all our changing needs. It is
the origin of every good and perfect gift. There is nothing
we can want or desire that does not ultimately proceed
from him.

*   *   *

It would be difficult to imagine anything less like our
own nature. We are never the same for two moments
together. We never continue in one stay. But no, that is
not altogether true. We are forgetting that there is in us
too a certain element of stability.

After all, we are his children. Of his own good will he brought us into existence. We take after our Father. And, if we reflect sadly how far we have lost that likeness, we must remind ourselves that, just because we have become so unlike him, he has caused us to be born again. Incredible as it may seem, 'of his own will begat he us with the Word of truth.'

That Word is the eternal Logos, his only-begotten Son. Through him he has planted the seed of a new personality within us, which, growing to maturity, will re-establish in us the likeness to him we have lost. We are intended to be the first-fruits of a new creation, an earnest of what all mankind may become as they yield to the influences of that same new birth.

So important does this thought seem to St. James that he returns to it: 'Receive with meekness the engrafted Word.' The New English Bible plays it down by translating 'Word' with a small w: 'Quietly accept the message planted in your hearts.' But that is to neglect the constant interplay between the spoken word and the Eternal Word, which is so remarkable a feature of the New Testament and which is so difficult to render into English.

* * *

In either case the Word or word must have its direct influence in our lives. It must restore us in the image of the Father, and it must revive in us something of his immutability. Anything like hysteria is out of place in the Christian life. We must not burst out into ill-considered speech, and certainly anger must be very slow to show itself in our work or acts.

The Christian must be teachable (swift to hear), quiet (slow to speak), gentle (slow to wrath). He must therefore avoid all that violence of language which is becoming more and more characteristic of our communications with each other to-day. 'What's in a word?' someone may ask. But a word is in itself a kind of act. The more accustomed we grow to violent words, the more prone do we become to violent acts. And below both word and act our minds grow accustomed to violent habits of thought.

This is the cause of much un-Christ-like talk and behaviour to-day. We must learn to cultivate the steady, quiet, unhesitating strength that comes straight from the immutable kindness of God. After all, that is our proper nature, and whatever is contrary to it, however common, is, in the true sense, unnatural.

ROGATION SUNDAY

Easter V   *St. James* I. 22

PRAYER in the first instance means simply 'asking.'
It goes on to imply converse, and finally communion,
with God.

In the first instance it is just asking. Quite simply we
ask God for what we want, like children approaching an
affectionate father. There are no elaborate thoughts about
whether we are asking too often or too much. Instinctively we know that, if what we ask is not likely to be good
for us, the request will not be granted. In that knowledge
we ask with all the greater confidence.

Of course this cuts the ground from under the feet of
the clever and humourless people who talk about the
absurdities of prayer. We shall be praying this week
especially for the right kind of weather. Everyone knows
that what may be the right kind for us may be the wrong
kind for somebody else. What does that matter? The
Father in heaven is quite capable of adjusting our neces-
sities to the needs of other members of his family. But
he does want us to confide to him our needs.

The only limit to our petitions is that they should be
made within the will of God.

*   *   *

Prayer becomes converse when there is an opportunity
for interchange between God and ourselves. It is the
running conversation that we carry on with God all day
and every day. It includes the ejaculatory prayer that
we utter at any moment, when answering the door,
when opening a letter, when greeting a friend, when
addressing a stranger, when starting a fresh piece of work

or beginning a meal. This is a two-way conversation because there is always the split second in which one may hear the word of advice or warning or encouragement.

More specifically this kind of conversation takes place when we deliberately devote some time to reading a passage of scripture and thinking about it before using the thoughts it arouses as a basis for prayer. There is no need to be more formal in our meditations than that. Even those who become adept at the most complicated procedures are glad at times to fall back on the simplest possible way of thinking over fundamental things in the presence of God.

Perhaps in this custom of converse with God should also be included our intercessions. After all they are our opportunity of talking to him about the needs of the world, both that part of it comprising our immediate environment and also that of which we have no personal experience, but about which we read and hear a great deal. They are all within the care of the King of the Universe, and as we are his sons we should be vitally interested in them all.

*   *   *

That brings us to the third type of prayer, which is communion. This condition 'transcends the imperfect offices of prayer and praise.' It is the comfortable silence that can only be enjoyed where those in each other's company are very close friends. Where such friendship does not exist, silence may become embarrassing. But how often do we read of a couple who have discovered a deep personal unity: 'Neither spoke; they had passed beyond the necessity for speech'?

Television was showing us the other evening the film of Charles de Foucauld's community in the North African desert. We may have noticed that, lonely as the situation

was, he had laid it down that each monk should spend
one day and night each month alone in complete solitude
away from all habitations, and that in addition there was
always one monk living a hermit's life at the top of the
mountain. And you may remember how the narrator
said that in that vast loneliness and amid the grandeur of
those mountain peaks it was impossible not to feel the
presence of God.

Well, that is a graphic and symbolic description of what
communion with God means. But it is not really necessary
to depart from the habitations of men in order to be
alone with God. Each man ought to carry a hermit's cell
in his own heart. To it he should be able to retire at any
moment, and find that essential openness with God which
is the very spirit of all true prayer.

THE SAVIOUR'S TRIUMPH

WHAT was the significance of the Ascension? First, it put the seal upon a mission accomplished.

The incarnate Son of God had fulfilled a threefold purpose. He had revealed the character of God in a unique and final way. He brought to a conclusion all the partial revelation through priest and law-giver and prophet. He had made men see God as the embodiment of fatherly affection, and he had shown in his own teaching and suffering how far the love of God could go.

He had at the same time made his own disciples realize that they must do their utmost to make this love the leading characteristic of their own lives. In the field of morals they must henceforth value everything from this point of view.

He had also inaugurated a new dispensation of special grace. Even in the moment when men were ready to fall into despair because they could not reach so high an ideal, they would realize that it was already accomplished within them. What they could not do of themselves God's grace and Spirit could and would do for them.

*   *   *

The second significance of the Ascension was that it manifested the Saviour's triumph. In Rome every great general returning victorious from the wars was accorded a public triumph. We have been accustomed in our own day to the sight of troops celebrating their victories in a special march through London. In the case of Jesus we must reckon that the vast welcoming crowds were in the courts of heaven. Nevertheless, even on earth there was a handful of disciples to feel the thrill of his triumphant return.

However we may explain it, it was a visible assurance to those who believed, that Christ's sufferings had not been in vain, but that he had returned to his Father. It was to them a guarantee that his work had been accepted and that all was in accordance with God's plan. In Christ's triumph they saw the forecast of their own: the victory would one day assuredly be theirs as it was now his.

There can be little doubt also that this dramatic return had its effect in the conversion of others. We know the recruiting value of the ceremonial marching of our own troops. There is no reason why we should not look for the same result in Jesus' triumph. It rounded off his earthly life as no other method of departure could. It revealed unmistakably the hand of God. It required faith to be accepted. But, for those who did accept it, it confirmed the whole revelation of the divine purpose for the universe.

*   *   *

The third significance of the Ascension was that it opened the way for the beginning of a new era.

There is the sending of the Spirit who, coming from the Father, takes Christ's place among us and keeps alive his revelation in our minds. This special help is not intended as something for us to cherish and keep for ourselves: it is to impel us to offer our own testimony in face of the world. We have to bear witness to Christ as he bore witness to his Father. His earthly mission is now over, but his Spirit is in us to enable us to understand it more completely and to express it more boldly.

This is not to be done without difficulty. We are warned that there will be opposition. In the past that meant sometimes cruel persecution, as indeed it has done once again for many Christians in our own day. But we are warned in advance precisely in order that when such difficulties do arise we shall not be unduly troubled by them.

To be forewarned is to be forearmed. Christ's triumph does not mean that we shall never need to brace ourselves to make a special effort or to show special courage. It means that the great decisive victory has been already won, and that, if we commit ourselves to it, we also shall share the victorious ascent to heaven.

DOMINION FOR EVER

THE feast of the Ascension brings us to the very heart and core of the New Theology.

The fact of the Ascension, as described in Luke and Acts, has long been under question both because of the alleged paucity of documentary evidence and because of inherent improbability. One would require, it is said, a great deal of contemporary witness before accepting a story of a bodily ascent into heaven.

To-day the attack centres upon the need for any such ascent at all. We have grown out of the childish belief that heaven is a place 'up there' beyond the stars. Mr. Khruschev says that his astronauts have been unable to find it. The old story of a three-storied universe, once held by theologian and scientist alike, has now been abandoned. So why cling to a view of the manner of Christ's passage from this earth which is evidently based upon the old theory? The question is obviously of present importance because it raises the issue whether we can still with good conscience observe the annual festival of the Ascension.

But there is another reason for its importance. The current view of the Ascension, we are told, is positively harmful because it distorts the proper view of God. We ought not to be thinking of God as 'up there' or 'out there'; we should be thinking of him as within our own personality, as, in fact, the ground of our being.

*   *   *

To the older objections we need not pay much attention. They rest essentially upon a view of Christ's resurrection body which is expressly excluded by the New Testament evidence. If Jesus' body, after he rose from the dead could behave as the New Testament says it did, then there is no difficulty in believing that he could rise visibly from the earth before the eyes of his disciples. Or, if one prefers to think that the post-resurrection appearances were 'veridical visions,' there is no reason why this last appearance and the manner of its ending should not belong in the same category.

What is more important is that we should meet the view that God is not 'without' but only 'within' the natural world. Such a view would, of course, be quite contradictory of traditional Christian teaching. Certainly the Church has never denied that God is 'within.' On the contrary, it has asserted most emphatically that he is 'closer to us than breathing, nearer than hands and feet.'

But it has also asserted with equal emphasis that he is 'without,' that he is not confined within the universe he has made but 'rules in highest heaven.' It is recognized that in speaking of God any spatial metaphors may be out of place, but the fact of utmost importance enshrined in the traditional teaching is that God is the creator and ruler of the universe: he is not somehow derived from it.

*   *   *

Actually this truth is suggested by the very term our new teachers are so fond of using. If God is the 'ground of our being,' then he is not only the source but the environment in which our being exists. He is external to it as well as internal. He is the soil from which the seed draws its life. In theological terms he is transcendent as well as immanent.

To this double truth we must bear witness. Whitsuntide will emphasize the second half of it, but the Ascension proclaims the first half, and one cannot let it go. It is the great guarantee that 'God's in his heaven, all's right with the world.'

No doubt we shall meet with opposition, but that is what Jesus promised us. The great thing is to know that we shall share his triumph, and that one day he will come again to claim his own.

WIND AND FIRE

IMAGINE the scene: the packed crowd of pilgrims up
for the feast; the Palestinian sun, of which T. E.
Lawrence said that 'it struck like a sword'; the waves of
heat quivering from walls and battlements.

And then the blessed relief of the mighty wind, 'the
rushing of a violent wind,' as J. B. Phillips translates it,
clearing the atmosphere, lifting the sultry pall, bringing
lightness and invigoration. Before it the rays of heat
dissolve, not disappearing altogether, but seen again (as
some afterwards told the story) as tongue-like jets of
flame above the head of each disciple. The apostles are all
strangely moved: they are filled with a new exhilaration:
they utter strange sounds, which are quickly interpreted
as words in foreign languages. Some of the bystanders
begin to laugh and say, 'They are just drunk.' Others are
moved to sympathy and see in this excitement a vivid
manifestation of the powerful Spirit of God.

There can be no doubt that in the apostolic church,
and even long after the apostles' time, this phenomenon,
which was so prominent on the first Whit-Sunday, and
which seems so strange to us, was regarded as one of the
commonest signs of possession by the Spirit. Indeed, it
was deemed quite sufficient of itself to guarantee a genuine
conversion to Christianity and to warrant immediate
baptism, where that rite had not already been performed.

*   *   *

The external marks of ecstasy were perhaps not particularly important in themselves. They were, however,

important as revealing an overwhelming sense of a
complete change in the life of the individual. That change
was something essential to the Christian religion: indeed,
it might be said with justice to be quintessential Christianity. It was a change from inertia to activity, from death
to life. It might be described either as incorporation into
Christ or as possession by the Spirit of Christ. Men were
alternatively said to be 'in Christ' or 'filled with the
Spirit.' We are reminded of the prayer of humble access:
'that we may evermore dwell in him and he in us.'

Of course, the phenomenon was psychological, but
Church and sacraments had their part to play in this
process of conversion. Incorporation into Christ implied
initiation into his body, the Church; and baptism, with
its complement in confirmation, was not only the cere-
mony of initiation but also the means by which converts
were filled with the Spirit. Long after Christian life had
assumed an aspect of routine and normality the phrases
remained to witness to the intimacy and ardour that should
characterize the relation of believers to their Lord in
every age. The fact that they have dropped out of normal
speech and that we have to go back to the Bible to recover
them shows how far present-day religion is removed from
the enthusiasm of our first forefathers in the faith.

*   *   *

The important thing is to remember that the two phrases
are in effect synonymous. To be in Christ is to be filled
with his Spirit. Such a thing as a nominal Christian
should not really be possible. If we have not the Spirit
of Christ, we are none of his; and if we have his Spirit,
we must be active members of his Church. Perhaps the
incisiveness of this message will come home to us if we
return for a moment to the symbols of the wind and the
fire.

In many languages wind, breath, spirit are all denoted by the same word. All alike imply a certain vitality, invigoration, alertness. A breath of fresh night air as one emerges from a crowded stuffy hall: how deeply one takes it into one's lungs and what refreshment it brings! So God breathed into man's nostrils the breath of life, and so the wind of God brought life to the re-clothed skeletons of Ezekiel's vision. Fire, similarly, has always been a symbol of zeal. How it runs through dry grass; how eager are its flames to reach to the next object; how terrible and how magnificent it can be! Is our life in the Spirit at all like that?

May this Whitsuntide bring to our jaded spirits 'new life, new love, new vigour, and new resolution that we may nevermore faint nor droop nor tire in our duty.'

AN ANALOGY IN OURSELVES

Trinity Sunday   *Revelation* 4. 1

WHEN we were small children busy with our arith-
metic lessons we were sometimes puzzled by the fact
that, although we got a right answer, we did not win the
approbation of our teacher. The reason, we were told,
was that we had used a wrong method. We were assured
that the rightness of our answer was a mere accident, and
that, if we wished to be sure of getting a correct solution
to our problem, we must always set about it in the right
way.

Trinity Sunday reminds us of this childish experience,
because it tells us that there is a right and a wrong way
of thinking about God. People are inclined to ask what
does it matter so long as we have the right attitude? If I
am ready to believe in him, to worship him and to obey
him, does it really matter how I define his person or his
attributes? The obvious reply is that, unless I think about
him in the right way, I cannot be sure of maintaining the
right attitude towards him.

Fortunately, in our generation, we no longer have to
face the taunts of those who used to make great play
with the impossibility of a 'three in one.' The science of
psychology, if it still remains in a tentative condition, has
nevertheless made clear the multiple character of the
human personality. If mystery is the characteristic note
of our own being, it must be still more the note of the
being of God.

*   *   *

The only response to mystery is faith. But sometimes
faith is helped by some analogous mystery in ourselves.

In the present instance we may even find a slight parallel to the mystery of God's being in our own individuality.

A little reflection makes us aware of a three-storied structure in our nature. There is at bottom the whole region of the unconscious, what the psychologists used to call the subliminal self—the self under the threshold. Above that there is the ordinary consciousness of everyday life when our senses and powers of reason are on the alert. And above that again is a height of consciousness which we reach in our most exalted moments, when we are 'outside ourselves' in worship, in joy, in the recognition of beauty, in fully creative thought.

So distinct are these three levels of consciousness that sometimes it is difficult to recognize oneself as the same person. Indeed, we know that in some individuals division is so sharp that they may to all intents and purposes move temporarily from one personality to another.

No one would say that this is an adequate picture of the multi-personality of God, but it does assuredly make it easier to realize that the teaching of the Athanasian Creed is not so incredible as so many of the publicists of the past generation thought it was.

*   *   *

Mystery then is met by faith. We recognize God as Creator in the formation of the universe, as Redeemer in the history of Jesus Christ, as Sanctifier in the constant influence of the Holy Spirit. In all three Persons we recognize one and the same God, constituting the whole universe and framing its operations so as to bring men to an ultimate share in his eternal bliss. All this we can see and accept.

But a mere act of acceptance is not enough. Faith does not end with itself. If it does not issue in worship, it has failed. If we truly recognize God, we must inevitably acknowledge his greatness. When Ezekiel saw him, he fell on his face in obeisance: when Jeremiah received his call he could only say, 'Ah, Lord God, I am but a child'; when Isaiah had his vision, he could only stammer out, 'I am a man of unclean lips.' In every case the perception of God reveals his greatness as contrasted with our littleness. This results in our appreciation of his worth: that is, in worship.

Mystery, faith, worship: it is a natural sequence. It is the proper progression by a right method to a correct conclusion. It is in faith that we adore the inscrutable mystery of the eternal Godhead, God in three Persons, blessed Trinity.

THE ROYAL LAW

'FAITH,' says St. James, 'without works is dead.'
A belief that does not issue in action is not faith but
mere opinion. So the second half of the Christian year is
devoted to the question of right conduct.

Having considered the events of Jesus' life and the
doctrines based upon them, we begin this Sunday to consider once again what should be their effect on our own
practical, everyday lives. In doing so we are brought
back sharply to the point from which we began, when we
first set ourselves to contemplate the Lord's coming.
The exhortation of Trinity I, 'Beloved, let us love one
another,' is as clear as the trumpet-call of Advent I,
'Owe no man anything, but to love one another.' It is the
royal law, the basic rule of Christian ethics.

In the epistle we are given three grounds for the recognition of this law: the character of God, the revelation
made by Christ, and practical expediency.

*   *   *

Fundamental is the fact that God himself is love. Here
being and attribute run into one. Love is not just a quality
of God, but God *is* love. All speculation as to the meta-
physical nature of the Absolute pales into comparative
insignificance beside the one overwhelming fact that God
is love—all love, so that whatever else we may say of him
takes its meaning from that fact. Even what may seem
to be his more terrible dealings with the human race are
dictated by his love, just as the cruel-seeming operation
of the surgeon is dictated by the necessity to save life.

29060

Even the Old Testament prophets were granted some vision of this exquisite reality. Hosea hovers between the love of the husband winning back an erring wife and that of a protective father for a small boy. 'How shall I give thee up, Ephraim?' 'When Israel was a child, then I loved him, and called my son out of Egypt.' 'I taught Ephraim to walk.' All the mighty acts of God were seen as illustrations of his affection for his own people, and this perception led to the interpretation of all history as a scheme of salvation.

*   *   *

In Jesus this love was revealed as an attitude not to Israel only but to all mankind. It was to be seen in Jesus' own character, in his acts, and in his teaching.

His character no doubt produced impatient reactions from some individuals as it did from Judas, and downright opposition from various parties and classes. But the Marys, the Peters, the Johns responded to the love they saw in him and began to recognize it as reflection of the nature of God.

Jesus' *acts* revealed this essential character, whether he was blessing little children, performing compassionate miracles of healing, meeting the needs of the hungry, or providing for the future of his mother.

His teaching echoed his practice. The law he gave in the Sermon on the Mount was in effect the golden rule. The character he sketched in the beatitudes was an analysis of love. He did not work out that analysis like a professor in the lecture-room, but he allowed the jewel of *agape*, his New Commandment, to be seen and understood by showing its different facets and letting the light of his own understanding play upon them. As a result his followers began to realize that for them the fundamental

rule of life must be the determined effort in all circumstances to seek the highest good of each and every person
with whom they came in contact.

*   *   *

If it was thus that 'the Father sent the Son to be the
Saviour of the world,' it was no less clear that in the long
run the observance of the rule of love was the best practical expedient. It was only this that could remove fear
and timidity and enable a man to walk in confidence.
If you were busy seeking the good of others, you had not
much opportunity for selfish emotions. To-day Nygren
has taught us to distinguish sharply between *agape* and *eros*.
Fr. D'Arcy has continued the lesson by showing that even
the lowliest manifestations of *eros* contain a germ that may
develop into the most sincere love of both God and man.
And Bertrand Russell has told us blushingly that the best
practical advice he can give the present generation is to
practise the virtue 'that the Christians call love.'

MARVEL NOT

IN every kind of competition it is good to know and
understand your opponent. In actual warfare it is
almost essential that a general should study the mind of
his enemy. It is perhaps for this reason that so early in
the Trinity season we are led to think as clearly as possible
about the enemy of the soul.

St. John has no doubt who our chief opponent is, and
he refers to him (or it) more frequently and in more
explicit terms than other New Testament writers. In his
view our great enemy is the 'world.' St. John sees the
Christian life as a prolonged struggle against the world.

Our difficulty is that the term 'world' is so often used
in a good sense. We know that in the beginning God made
the world and he saw that it was good. How then are we
to regard it as our enemy? The fact is that in St. John's
use of the term it means more than the actual physical
world. It is applied to society, and in this kind of context
it implies a particular aspect of society, society organized
apart from God. To St. John the world generally means
men and women who acknowledge no genuine allegiance
to God.

The paradoxical feature of this kind of world is that
it is not altogether outside us. There is something in all
of us that is in rebellion against God. The enemy is
within our own gates. But, when we become truly
Christian in heart and mind, we enter into a new life
in which we set ourselves to overcome the world whether
within us or outside.

*   *   *

We can now understand why St. John tells us not to be surprised if we find that the world hates us. It is not nice to feel oneself hated by anybody. But, life being what it is, we must expect to have opponents who fight against the ideals we have received and by which we try to live. And, because these ideals are the very opposite of those entertained by these men, their dislike sometimes turns to actual hatred.

In any case hatred is characteristic of the world in this sense. For the Christian, hatred of other people is impossible: it is quite outside his nature. His guiding principle is love. Like his Saviour, the Christian must wish all men to be saved. Origen, the great second-century speculative theologian, surmised that the all-conquering love of God would eventually convert and save even Satan himself.

'Marvel not, my brethren, if the world hate you.' In our own immediate surroundings we find hatred expressing itself not so much in open and avowed opposition or active persecution as in apathy and neglect.

*   *   *

We return to the thought that there is something of the world even in our hearts. Are we consistently loving to our own fellows? This is where conscience makes cowards of us all. It is not that we have actually persecuted others, but, if neglect of God implies actual hatred, does not the same apply to our neglect of our fellowmen?

It will not do just to plead ignorance. Someone has said that unawareness is the great sin. We should be aware of the need both on our door-step and also in the regions overseas. Our love should embrace the undernourished millions as well as the member of our own household in need of sympathy and help. We must decide whose side we are on, that of the Master who left his high estate to live as a servant among men, or that of the world for which hatred is a necessary part of its psychology. Who can have an entirely clear conscience in such a matter? Yet, if conscience does condemn us, we must not be morbid about it. 'God is greater than our heart and knoweth all things.' So long as our initial determination remains and we are genuinely trying to live by the law of love, he will guide us into fuller understanding, and give us grace to approximate more nearly to the truth as he has revealed it in Christ Jesus. So shall we not be conformed to this world but be transfigured by the constant renewing of our inner life.

THE STABLE COMMUNITY

P. T. FORSYTH used to teach his students to preach not from isolated texts but, as he said, 'from whole paragraphs.' This has often been our method in our reflections on the epistles, and the style will suit us admirably to-day.

We remember that St. Peter is addressing the entire Christian community over a wide area, and that in face of a threatened persecution he is trying to build them up into a strongly integrated body. He asks them to think about their common order, their common cause, and their common calling.

The common order is terribly important, for if they are not a well-knit community they will never be able to stand the rigours of persecution. The way to achieve such unity is, first, to practise humility in their dealings with each other. They must not be proud or overbearing, but they must be prepared for a great deal of 'give and take.' God is their common master and in subjecting themselves to him they must be prepared to perform whatever task, however lowly, is accorded to them within the community.

A further necessary way to secure such order is to take care not to panic. In spite of all that threatens they must not be over-anxious. Undue anxiety will make them incapable of consistent effort. They must remember that they are in God's hands and that he will take care of them.

*   *   *

Having thus indicated the kind of spirit that can produce good order St. Peter reminds his readers of their common cause. This includes a common enemy to fight, a common discipline to maintain, and a common knowledge that they share the present situation not only among themselves in the local churches of Asia Minor, but also with Christians throughout the whole Roman Empire. It is a 'global' situation.

Their common enemy is the devil himself, the author of all evil. He is pictured as a lion in the amphitheatre, stirred up by the shouts of the crowd, roaring his hunger and his defiance, waiting to pounce upon the first victim driven to him in the arena.

We do not normally think of evil in this open guise. Usually we picture it as a much more subtle force whose presence must first be detected before it can be definitely resisted. But there are times when evil stalks abroad open and undisguised. Then we have to ask for the simple courage to meet it undismayed.

The surest way to subdue it is not to be taken by surprise. We must be sober and vigilant, like a good athlete always in training to meet any sudden demand. Above all we must be ready to resist in faith, having a complete trust in God that whatever may be the changing fortunes of the present he will ultimately lead us out into victory and peace.

* * *

Finally, the thought of the common order and the common cause is joined by the thought of the common calling. It is surprising that St. Peter puts the calling last, but it comes like a blessing at the conclusion of a service. 'The God of all grace who hath called you into his eternal glory by Christ Jesus.' The end of our warfare is to be triumphal victory—not just success on the field of battle but a resounding home-coming for all the world to see. It is to the triumph no less than to the battle that we are called.

H

The intervening trial will be short. It will strengthen our manhood, and make us the kind of men God wants us to be—mature and reliable. 'Make you perfect, stablish, strengthen, settle you.' The words breathe an atmosphere of calm, unperturbed competence. Such men know how to deal with life. They are prepared for any eventuality and are never caught unawares.

The spirit of the whole passage seems concentrated in the last phrase 'settle you.' It means to build upon a sure foundation and is the same word as is used of the house 'founded' upon a rock. Jesus is the sure foundation on which we can all rest secure and immovable. His is our cause, in him is our well-ordered life, and he it is who guarantees both to the individual and to the community the ultimate perfection to which we are called.

THE FINAL CHANGE

DO you ever think about the end of the world? If so, how do you envisage it? The scientists are not much help. They dispute whether it will come about through overmuch expansion or excessive contraction; whether a clash of planets will cause it to dissolve in fervent heat or a change of epochs bring in a new and completely devastating glacial age.

Although some of the phrases in which these views are expressed are reminiscent of the Bible, the scriptures are not greatly interested in the scientific point of view. What they are certain about is that there will come a day when God's rule will be openly accepted by all that exists, and that that acceptance will bring an unending age of universal bliss. The author of the Apocalypse thinks that before this can happen the present earth and heaven will have to be removed and a new heaven and earth brought in.

St. Paul, as we see in to-day's epistle, looks forward to the same essential end, but he views its process somewhat differently. He does not picture the present material universe as subject to annihilation. He prefers to think of it as destined to be changed.

*   *   *

St. Paul bases his conclusion on the belief that 'there is now no condemnation to them that are in Christ Jesus.' Our unity with Christ through the Spirit has delivered us from our bondage to corruption, has eradicated the seed of decay from our whole personality, body as well as soul, and has given us the guarantee of immortality and bliss.

In this happy condition creation itself shares. It is true that everything was made subject to the same disabilities, such as suffering and death, as man himself inherits. But in the case of the rest of existence it was not through its own fault. Man made a deliberate choice: the rest of the created universe was put in the same condition in order to give man a chance of working his passage home— of acquiring the kind of character that alone can make him a fit companion for God through eternity. When man has accepted the conditions of his salvation, then and only then will the universe be set free to enjoy his new life with him.

At present, however, the whole creation groans and travails in pain together. It is under the curse that fell upon it on account of Adam's transgression. 'Cursed is the ground for thy sake.' It does not matter if there were death and calamity in the world before man appeared. Everything was arranged before the beginning to consort with the destiny of man. The universe was made to share in anticipation our fallen condition in order that it might provide a fitting environment for our recovery.

*   *   *

It follows that although we all, men and the universe together, suffer grievously from time to time, our pains are not death-throes but the pangs of birth. We have already enjoyed a foretaste of that new life in our consciousness of oneness with Christ. That is itself the first-fruits of the Spirit, an earnest of the glory to come.

This knowledge should give us courage as we face life's ordeal. It prevents us from thinking that we are the puppets of an inexorable fate, or the mere sport of chance.

There is a plan for the universe and even the less pleasant experiences of everyday life are covered by it.

This teaching of St. Paul's also gives us confidence for the future. Whatever we suffer now, it is quite infinitesimal compared with the immensity of the glory in which we shall one day participate.

There is really no wastefulness in God's plan. Although all is arranged to promote man's good, the created universe, when it has performed its function, will not be forgotten or neglected. 'Not one life shall be destroyed, or cast as waste upon the void, when he hath made the pile complete.' We and the universe together shall share in the ultimate restoration and God will be all in all.

THE GOOD LIFE

WE are accustomed to find moral codes incorporated
in the epistles of St. Paul. In some respects this
first epistle of St. Peter is a kind of prolonged moral code:
so much so indeed that some modern scholars have come
to believe that it was originally written, not as a letter
at all, but as a homily addressed to candidates for baptism
and confirmation. It was intended to describe to them
the moral characteristics of the good, the Christian, way
of life.

Thus our portion of it, which is set as the epistle for to-
day, begins with an exhortation to true courtesy. Christians cannot all expect to think alike, but they should all
'have one mind', that is they should all recognize the same
purpose. They are all seeking the same end, so they can
afford to defer to each other in love.

It is obvious that if they are in that frame of mind they
will never be tempted to use bad language to each other.
They will be gentle and kind. Their humblemindedness
will keep them from any thought of violence either in
word or deed.

In any case they should remember that they were made
Christians precisely in order that they might 'inherit a
blessing.' They must learn to distribute their legacy
and to become a centre of blessing for others.

*   *   *

Like many another writer and speaker St. Peter here
clinches his argument with a quotation. It is a section of
a hymn on the good life, reminiscent of the description in

the book of Deuteronomy of the difference between the two ways of life and death.

> Whoever loves life and would see good days,
> Must restrain his tongue from evil
> And his lips from deceit.

The verse goes on to explain that one of the incentives to this special care is that 'the eyes of the Lord are over the righteous.' This sentiment has a somewhat dubious sound to us. We were taught when we were children that God's eye is always upon us, and it was said with the intention of making us afraid. Its overtone of threat still rings in our ears.

It is true that God looks with displeasure on all that is wrong. We must not be so 'modern' as to disguise that fact from ourselves. But the reason why it is stated here that God's eye is upon us is to encourage us to recognize that God constantly watches us and reads even our inmost thoughts, not to blame, but to praise.

One of the 'ancient' Friendly Societies still has the all-seeing eye of God as part of its emblem. The intention is not to frighten us but to give us confidence in the divine ordering of all things. Nothing happens without God's knowledge, and God will see that no real harm comes to his children.

*   *   *

So having sketched his moral code and having given the reason why it should be scrupulously observed, St. Peter goes on to reassure his readers as to the happy frame of mind they will enjoy if they follow his advice.

It is very unlikely, he says, that anyone will ever want to harm them if they are devoted to doing what is good. But even if someone is so evilly disposed as that, they must rest confident that God will see them right in the end.

Here it is an interesting question whether the writer is thinking merely of the possibility of ill-tempered neighbours or whether he is thinking of the more sinister threat of official persecution. In either case his point remains the same: God will look after his own, and there is no need for his children to be afraid.

Indeed, if they suffer, not for any evil but for the good they have done, such as their profession of Christianity or their effort to show Christian neighbourliness to others, then they ought to be happy rather than sorry. They will at least be following in the footsteps of their Master who did no sin and yet was put to a cruel death.

Their consolation will be that through sharing his experiences they will be able to enthrone the Lord Christ more securely in their hearts. And if they are one with him in his apparent defeat, they will certainly be one with him in his ultimate triumph.

All this is included in the idea of incorporation into Christ.

WHAT CHRISTIANITY MEANS

IF you were asked to state in a short phrase what Christianity means, how would you answer? It would not be sufficient to say that it is some sort of creed, or mode of worship, or system of morals. All of these would be true, but they would not touch the real essence of our religion; much less would they be comprehensive. Perhaps the best phrase we could use would be 'incorporation into Christ.'

That at least is what St. Paul seems to assert at some length in to-day's epistle. He evidently thinks that the believer is so united with Christ that he recapitulates in himself the story of the life of Christ. Just as the embryo is said to recapitulate in itself the successive stages of human life before its actual birth, so we repeat in the new man that is born in us the birth, death, resurrection of Christ.

When we are baptized we share in Christ's death. Our old self is crucified with him, dies to the world. But we are also joined with Christ in his resurrection. We are the subjects of a new birth and rise with him to a new and more complete life. It is not that our own individuality is destroyed, but it is changed in virtue of our unity with Christ.

*   *   *

Now it is sometimes complained that such a view of the Christian life implies a condition merely static, outside the sphere of action, and consequently outside the sphere of morality altogether. But supposing we think of God as the 'God who acts,' not merely as universal, stationary being, but as pure act, one whose essence and whose action are identical. Then to be united with him is not a question of *being* only, but of energy and moral force.

To be joined to God in Christ, to be made partaker of his nature, does not mean just resting in an eternal quiescence, but a continual striving upwards and onwards. Life is a constant movement. When there is no possibility of movement, death supervenes. God is life. He is absolute perfection within which there is infinite opportunity for movement and progress.

We are dead to the world but alive to God through Jesus Christ. We have turned our back upon the world of darkness and our faces to the light. No doubt we do sometimes glance back over our shoulder, but we know how foolish that is, and we turn again to concentrate our attention upon the goal of our striving. We have the comfort of knowing that this is no despairing effort. It is not even pulling against the collar. It is in line with our true nature in Christ Jesus. We came from God, we go to God and we are in God.

*　　　*　　　*

It is this unity with Christ that ensures the continuance of our moral endeavour. It is really a question of what we most want. No doubt we want health and wealth, success and the esteem of our friends. But are these the things we want most, or are they all subservient to our love of God and our desire to please him?

Everyone who has ever loved knows the almost painful desire to link one's personality with that of the beloved. It is almost as if one wished for absorption each into the other. Paradoxically, although absorption is not possible, unity is. And the mere desire leaves us with a heightened sense of fulfilment of our individual being through the relationship of near-union with each other.

What we truly desire is to have the same mind that is in Christ Jesus. We find our longing for holiness strengthened by our contact with him. We know that our prospect of ultimately attaining it is guaranteed by his life in us. We are conscious that we are already in potentiality dead indeed unto sin but alive unto God through Jesus Christ our Lord. And we rely upon the gradually developing maturity of that new life in us to bring us finally to such good things as pass man's understanding.

All this is included in the idea of incorporation into Christ.

THE TWO WAYS

ST. PAUL, who is often content to give his instruction on morals merely in short lists of virtues and vices, here extends his scope to give a reasoned description of the doctrine lying behind his particular code.

He confesses that he is using language adapted to the special condition of his hearers. They understand very well what is meant by slavery, how the slave is entirely at the mercy of his master and must do precisely what is ordered. Well, both goodness and wickedness are a kind of servitude. If you change masters, you are still under obedience; but how different can the conditions of service be! Under one master you hate the whole business on which he is engaged and detest every moment of your allotted task. Under another you are full of admiration for the work he is doing and are proud to assist him in every detail.

At the same time one has to remember that the second demands as faithful service as the first. You cannot be neglectful or half-hearted simply because you have a good and kind master. You must give yourself as whole-heartedly in love to the second as in fear to the first.

*   *   *

Many thinkers have asked what is the source of the slavery under which mankind labours. It is to be noticed that when the term slavery is used in a moral sense it practically always refers to a bondage to evil and not to good. It is generally agreed that the cause of the compulsion must lie very deep in human nature.

The old Hebrews used to trace it to a kind of 'evil imagination' that stirred within the mind of men and led ultimately to overt acts of shame. Later they seem to have thought of it as planted within the character by some invisible enemy in the spiritual sphere. Christians have generally thought of it as a taint that has corrupted an originally good human nature.

Whatever the source, it is universally agreed by all sorts and conditions of men that the taint is there, and that if one did not take care one might become just as much a slave to its corruption as the alcoholic and the drug addict become the slaves of a physiological obsession.

It is from this bondage that Paul congratulates his readers on having been freed. 'You once yielded your bodies to the service of impurity and lawlessness, resulting in moral anarchy; now you must yield them to the service of righteousness, making for a holy life.'

*   *   *

So from considering the source St. Paul turns to consider the end. Curiously he uses the symbolism of wages. A slave does not usually receive wages: he works not for an agreed award but from sheer necessity. However, St. Paul says that in this case the master Sin will pay a wage. And what is that wage? Not merely moral anarchy, but actual death. As so often, Paul draws no distinction between the death of the body and the death of the soul. Dissoluteness may easily result in the death of the body, but most certainly, if left unchecked, it will result in the death of the finer elements of the individual personality.

Against such an end one has to set the wages of holiness. But this is not really a wage; it is not some *quid pro quo* payment, a proportionate reward for so many hours of labour. It is a sheer gift, something we have not earned or deserved, but a free bestowal of eternal life. And that life is as high in quality above normal life as eternity is above the mere passage of time.

This supreme gift comes to us through Jesus Christ our Lord. It is in our obedience to him and our firm union with him that we have the promise of a share in that life which is already his. This grand and glorious hope is more than sufficient justification for the devoted service to which we are bound here on earth.

THE SONS OF GOD

THE Bible has three stages by which it symbolizes the soul's upward ascent to God. The first and lowest is that of the servant.

There are two divisions even in this lowest stage. The term 'servant' covers two different kinds of service, that of the slave and that of the domestic. The characteristic of the slave is that he serves from the motive of fear. He has nothing to gain: he is not a person, even in the eyes of the law; he is merely a chattel, to be broken in a fit of anger and to be thrown away when its usefulness is over. Yet it is noteworthy that even St. Paul is proud to describe himself as the slave of Christ.

The domestic, the hired servant, is in a very different case. His characteristic is that he serves not from fear but from expectation of reward. He has a dignity and a self-respect that are denied to the other. He knows his value, and the good servant will take care that he fully earns his wages.

It is sometimes said that the Old Testament period was a necessary stage in the education of the people of God, first as slaves, then as servants, moving from fear to the hope of reward. So it is also said that there must always be an element of asceticism in all true religion, and that Puritanism is a valuable training for a Catholic.

*   *   *

The second main stage in the development of the Christian character is that of the friend. Our Lord himself said to his disciples: 'Henceforth I call you no longer servants, but I have called you friends.'

It is a tremendous change when one passes out of the servants' hall to take an honoured place in the drawing-room. One's whole status is altered. Jesus said that the great difference was that, while the servant need not know what was in the master's mind at all, the friend was a confidant to whom all knowledge of the Master's plans could be entrusted.

Three characteristics can be predicated of a friend: affection, understanding, freedom. Obviously there can be no real friendship without affection. Christ came to reveal God's friendship for men, to remove thoughts of punishment and payment from the minds of God's people and to awaken in them thoughts of love.

In this state of mind we are anxious to understand God. We recognize that he has placed us in an environment where, once we have learned the secret, everything speaks to us of him. Church and world; Bible and art; history and science; the light in men's eyes and the happiness in their voices—all alike tell us more of him and his ways.

This recognition gives us a new and exquisite sense of freedom. We are no longer bound to a harsh, unbending law. We are friends of the family and we move freely over the whole domain. Scrupulosity has no place in our thoughts or attitude. We are intimates of the owner. We are free of the whole house and grounds.

*   *   *

The third state is that of sons. And that brings us to to-day's epistle. 'As many as are led by the Spirit of God, they are the sons of God.' There is any amount of evidence in the New Testament that God does indeed offer us the almost incredible privilege.

Of course we are all the sons of God in the sense that he is responsible for our existence and that he constantly cares for us. But the Christian is adopted into a special relation to him, just as is the legally adopted son in any British family. The atmosphere of the family in which he grows up enters into the very fibre of the being of the adopted child; so we who have dropped the slavish spirit of fear have the Holy Spirit of God in our hearts causing us to think of God, and instinctively to address him, by the term implying a blood-relationship.

How close a relationship that is we can only appreciate by recognizing that it puts us on a certain level with Christ himself. He welcomes us into his own brother-hood: we share his fortunes with him: and we have the guarantee that one day we shall share with him his glory.

I

NEVER PRESUME

TO-DAY'S epistle is a lesson against presumption on
the part of Christian people. They are not to think
that because of their privileged position they are relieved
of the duty of trying to be good. Religious observance is
no substitute for morality.

St. Paul enforces the lesson by discussing the continuity of God's plan for salvation as revealed in the course
of history. In the Old Testament period the Jewish people
had been placed in much the same kind of privileged
position as the Christians enjoy now. Yet they fell from
the moral ideal expected of them and had to be punished.

The Jews even had their own parallel to the Christian
sacraments. They were all baptized in the cloud and in
the sea. That is to say, they all marched through the
wilderness under the Shekinah, the luminous cloud of
God's glory, and they were all saved through their
miraculous crossing of the Red Sea—a double symbol of
baptism.

Similarly, as a forerunner of the Eucharist, they had
eaten of the manna and drunk from the rock that Moses
had split in the desert, which, according to the Rabbinic
legend, had rolled after them with its continuing
supply of spring water. Yet in spite of these privileges the
people had given way to idolatry and its immoral
accompaniments.

*   *   *

History, as we say, repeats itself. Paul is convinced that,
whatever different forms it may take, God's essential
method remains the same. There is even a sense in which

these early forefathers of the Jewish race were sinning against Christ, although he was not born upon earth as Jesus of Nazareth until twelve or fifteen hundred years later.

Christ was existent from all eternity in the spiritual sphere; and, although they may not have known it, when they sinned they were really sinning against him. And what made their fault worse was that Christ was in effect the mysterious Rock which provided the necessary nourishment for their daily life. It was against this gracious influence that they rebelled.

How far St. Paul regarded this as sober history and how far as deliberate allegory we may not know. But we can understand his thought well enough to recognize how much store he set by the continuity of God's dealing with his children. All this, he might have said, is not just past history. It is not over and done with. It is a sharp reminder of our position to-day.

*   *   *

It does not matter that in point of fact the world has already continued nearly two thousand years since the coming of Christ. It is true that that is a good deal longer than the period between the coming of Christ and the wilderness wanderings at the dawn of the Hebrew people. The fact is that God's ways are still the same. He works by the sacramental principle. He uses outward and visible signs to convey to us his inward and spiritual grace. The cloud and the Red Sea are the precursors of baptism as the manna and the spring water are of the Eucharist.

But human nature remains essentially the same, too. As the wandering Jews gave way to sordid desires and betrayed the God who had shown them such kindness, so also may we, if we do not learn by the example of the past. The greater our privilege, the greater our responsibility. Don't presume on your position. Let him that thinketh he standeth take heed lest he fall.

So far we have not been tested beyond endurance. And always God provides the means by which we can get the better of our temptations. He is the same yesterday, to-day and for ever. We must see to it that we rest happy and secure in his stability; and we must never let our natural tendency to murmur and complain lead us into forgetfulness of that fact. Otherwise we may share the fate of those who were not allowed to enter the Promised Land.

GIFTS OF THE SPIRIT

IF you had asked a Churchman of the first generation
what was the characteristic sign of a Christian, he
would probably have answered, 'Possession of the Spirit
of Jesus.'

It was by the possession of that Spirit that Christians
recognized each other. It was the sure evidence that a
convert had passed the great divide that separated Jew
and pagan alike from the Christian world.

The presence of the Spirit was often manifested in a
special type of enthusiastic worship, in which the members
would fall into ecstasy and practise what was known as
'speaking with tongues.' But that was soon superseded,
and the presence of the Spirit was more commonly
recognized in the display of gentle and practical virtues
such as love, joy, peaceableness.

Always it was recognized that it was the power of the
Spirit that had brought conviction and made such
change of life possible. It was only the Spirit who could
spur the will to action.

*   *   *

St. Paul found it necessary to insist upon the unity of
this Spirit. The Christian calling manifested itself in so
great a variety of ways that a stranger might have thought
that different spirits were at work. Particularly easy
would such a thought be in a pagan environment where
nearly every variety of place and function was believed
to have its own god, where for instance there were different
gods for the hearth and the threshold as well as for luck and

for childbirth. But, the apostle says, all that is good in the spirit of man is an expression of the one divine Spirit of Jesus.

Over a large area of Queensland where irrigation is badly needed water is obtained by sinking sub-artesian bores. Deep underground there is a vast lake, the accumulation of centuries of rainfall. Its life-giving waters are tapped and run into channels so as to bring fruitfulness to many thousands of otherwise barren acres. However varied may be the channel and the resultant crop, it is always the effect of the one great subterranean lake.

So all good gifts flow from the self-same Spirit. There are differences of administration: that is, many different opportunities of service. There are differences of operation; that is, many different types of work. Life, as we know it, offers a vast variety of opportunity, but the skill and energy and willingness to do all for the glory of God and for the benefit of our fellows are always the inspiration of the one Holy Spirit.

*　　　*　　　*

As the channels differ, so also do the fruits that are the results of their life-giving stream. The epistle tells us that each man can profit in his own way from the manifestation of the one Spirit. St. Paul enumerates nine different activities as examples. They fall easily into three groups: personal, public and congregational.

The personal ones are wisdom, knowledge and faith. They are the interior gifts of character that are necessary to sustain any prolonged and successful effort. It is good to dwell on their meaning in our private thoughts, and realize that they *will* be given us if we ask for them.

The second group are the public ones, the out-going virtues, that bear witness of the Christian life to those who are outside: capacity to help others in their sufferings (healings), ability to exercise a strong psychological influence (miracles), a capacity of insight with boldness to speak the truth (prophecy). All these make a great impact upon the unbelieving world.

And then there are the gifts that are best understood by our fellow-members and are useful in worship: the capacity to judge between good and bad in the spiritual sphere, a gift for inspiring utterance, a power of understanding and interpreting to each other people of different enthusiasms. All are of great value in building up the one body of Christ. This new life, wherever or however it expresses itself, is all under control of the one and self-same Spirit of Christ, which is freely given to those who ask.

FIRST PRINCIPLES

CORINTH was a quarrelsome city. And its newly formed church had not wholly freed itself from the common characteristic. Of that we have evidence not only from St. Paul's letters but also from other Christian writing outside the New Testament.

The best way to keep the Christian community together was to bring its members back to first principles. So Paul reminds them of the preaching he had first given them. He had then emphasized three fundamental points: Christ's death, his resurrection, and the grace that came as a result of both.

First, let there be no doubt that Jesus had really and truly died. The scriptures had always said that he would; and furthermore he had been actually buried. This solemn iteration of the physical fact of the death was made necessary because some were already beginning to teach that it was altogether below the dignity of the Son of God to die. Either he who was tortured on the cross and laid in Joseph's tomb was a phantom, or someone else, such as Simon of Cyrene, was substituted for him.

So Paul emphasizes the death, not in order now to draw from it any doctrinal significance (except to say that it was 'for our sins'), but merely to assure his readers that, as there was a physical death, so there was a physical resurrection.

*   *   *

That there was a physical resurrection is guaranteed by the longest list of appearances, six in all, that we have in the New Testament. Paul includes the appearance to himself among the rest. However, he stresses that he is not relying only on his own experience, but also upon the tradition that he had received when he first joined the Christian Church.

Nevertheless he is so certain of his own vision of the risen Christ that elsewhere he bases upon it his claim to be an apostle. 'Am I not an apostle: have I not seen the Lord?' He obviously thinks of his encounter with Christ as being of the same pattern as those of the others who had seen him immediately after his resurrection.

Indeed, it had had the same effect of producing upon him an overwhelming sense of unworthiness as the perception of God's presence had brought long ago to the prophets Isaiah and Jeremiah, and later to Peter when he saw the miracle performed by Jesus. It was a strange mingling of humility and pride. 'I am an apostle and yet the least of all the apostles, a very runt of an apostle. But it is by the special grace of God that I am an apostle at all.'

*　　　*　　　*

Thus, having established the historical facts, Paul reminds the Corinthians of their effect in the moral and spiritual sphere. The result of this death and resurrection of Christ had been to make available in a newer and fuller measure for the believer God's grace; that is to say, his personal, freely given, assistance.

Paul had to argue on two fronts. The Jews were inclined to think of a resurrection body as being in effect very like the material body. The Greeks thought of the body as the prison of the soul, and expected it to be discarded entirely at death. Paul maintained that there was a resurrection body in some way continuous with this body, but a spiritualized body without the limitations that belong to life on this material plane.

Under the new conditions the risen Christ had communicated himself to St. Paul. The Christ-history of death and resurrection had resulted for him in an access of new capacity and vitality. Paul felt himself a new man, the instrument of a mighty power. Christ was in him, the hope of glory.

This was the original Christian message. It was the common experience of true believers. In it was to be found the guarantee of present unity and ultimate salvation. It is still the essence of the gospel for us to-day.

OUR SUFFICIENCY

ST. PAUL is here treating one of his basic themes, in
fact *the* basic theme of all his Christian theology. It is
that God has dealt with the world under two dispensations,
an old and a new. The dividing line came with the
Incarnation, with the life, death and resurrection of
Jesus Christ.

He is led into the discussion because he has to justify
the claim he has made to the Corinthians that he has a
right to advise them in religious matters. Do they expect
him to produce some written credentials to guarantee his
authority? He does not intend to do any such thing,
though presumably he could have produced some
authorization from the mother church in Jerusalem if he
had wished to do so.

Nor will he claim that he has any special gifts or
qualifications of his own that would make him out as an
obviously authoritative Christian leader. No, his suffi-
ciency is of God and of God alone. He makes his claim
in full reliance upon God through Christ. He has a
secure inner conciousness that God has called him to
be a minister of his new agreement with his chosen people.
He will now go on to explain the nature of that covenant.

*   *   *

On such a subject one cannot expect from Paul a
carefully balanced statement. The convert's reaction
against his old beliefs is generally of a violence proportionate to the strength with which they were held before
the change came. St. Paul is no exception. As the light
that shone into his eyes on that Damascus road blinded

him to everything else, so the illumination of his mind with regard to God's fresh ordering of mankind made all previous experience seem dark in comparison.

He does not deny that God had a scheme under the old dispensation, but it was a hard scheme, a matter of the meticulous keeping of a minutely detailed law. That at least is how it now appeared to Paul. He had himself done everything possible to be faithful to that scheme. He had distinguished himself as one of the foremost persecutors of those who had rebelled against it. But even in the midst of his strongest effort he knew at last that he had failed. He was overwhelmed by the entirely different character of the One whose followers he was seeking to put to death.

He saw now that no effort of his own could ever save him. He must accept the claim of the Christ that to be saved you must give up your adult confidence in your own strength and become as a helpless child. This was the meaning of the new dispensation. With Christ God had introduced a new method. You must recognize that you had no strength of yourself to help yourself; you cannot even think anything of yourself. Like an infant not yet able to talk or walk, you must just accept what you are given.

*　　　*　　　*

That is what equipped Paul as a competent minister of the new dispensation: he recognized the vital difference between the two psychologies and with a full heart accepted the new.

He was not going to say that there was nothing fine in the old. Did not the old story tell how Moses, when he received the law of the old dispensation, had such a glowing countenance that people were dazzled by it and he was compelled to wear a veil?

If such splendour could attend the coming of the old law, which was full of threats and penalties and death, was not the offer of the new gift of life and health in response to simple faith and trust far more glorious? One would recognize the contrast at once if one had ever experienced the change. No more fears, no more scrupulosity, no more dread of suffering or of death, no more terror of everlasting damnation.

Why not then take God at his word? Why not rest upon him in love and trust? Christ has opened the way. To follow him into this new age is like stepping from darkness into light, from death into life.

TWO ATTITUDES

TO St. Paul's way of thinking there were two alternative attitudes with which an earnest man might face
the world. The one was that of the honest, sober, indus-
trious citizen who knows his own value and is prepared to
demand a due recognition of it from his employer, but is
always conscious of the dire consequences that will
follow upon any dereliction of duty.

The other was that of a man who is not conscious
that the world owes him anything. He is aware only of
fundamental failure deep within himself. He feels that
he is so far from attaining even his own ideals that he
would never be able to repay God, whatever he managed
to accomplish, for the mere privilege of being alive.

St. Paul pondered a good deal over this difference;
all the more because it seemed to correspond to a change
that had taken place in his own life. He had once been
like the first man, and he had later become like the
second.

*   *   *

On fuller reflection St. Paul was led to see that this
personal experience was not something peculiar to himself. He saw it exemplified in the history of his nation.
It had its counterpart in the two successive dispensations
under which the Jews had been called to live.

At the beginning of Jewish history God had promised
that he would make Abraham and his descendant (that
is, one individual representing the whole people) a blessing
to the world. But things had gone wrong and the nation
had to be disciplined by being put under a rigid system

of law. The law was meant to make people realize not only what was the ideal manner of life, but also how difficult it was to live up to it.

While this period of severe training persisted the promise was in abeyance, but when it was over God fulfilled his promise to Abraham by sending his Son into the world to introduce a new dispensation, that of his Kingdom. Those who entered the Kingdom were not expected to live in a timorous spirit under a system of law but in the free, gracious spirit in which the original promise was made and received.

The difference in the quality of the two dispensations could be seen in that, whereas the promise was communicated by God directly, the law was administered only by angels as God's agents. The inference is that higher dignity and worth belong to the dispensation of promise, with which God deals personally.

*   *   *

In a good deal of this St. Paul may seem to us to be arguing like a Jewish rabbi. We get back in touch with him again when we realize what an effect he believed this change from law to promise had on a man's character.

The fundamental difference, to use our Lord's own metaphor, was the change from the status of a servant to that of a friend. The servant, even the good servant, enjoys nothing like the freedom of a friend of the family. The servant is dependent on his service for his livelihood and therefore is much more likely to be conscious both of the danger of losing his job and of the obligations that the adequate performance of his duties lays upon his employers. He is therefore much more likely to be subject to alternate fits of superiority and despondency.

The friend, on the other hand, accepts favours as a free gift. Even if he renders great services, he does not do so from hope of reward. His life is not lived from the point of view of equal pay for equal work. He knows that whatever he receives comes from his friend's good will. He therefore has no room to be either proud or patronizing. He carries no chip on his shoulder: he deserves nothing and receives all. His whole aim in life is to be friendly.

St. Paul has no doubt which is the finer character, and this Sunday's epistle contains the argument to prove his point.

FRUIT OF THE SPIRIT

'FRUIT OF THE SPIRIT' is a beautiful and expressive phrase. It takes us straight to the heart of Christian spirituality. It reveals that the holiness we so much desire is not something that can be gained by painful striving, but must grow simply and naturally out of the life that is within.

That life is nothing less than the Spirit of Christ. He communicates himself to the individual Christian and remains an abiding presence in the heart of the believer revealing his character in the thoughts, words, acts of his host. 'The righteous shall flourish as the palm-tree,' and the palm-tree grows (though this may not have been the original point of the text) from within outwards.

*   *   *

Something of this can be seen from the very order in which the 'fruits' are enumerated. They fall naturally into three sets of three, starting from the inward disposition and ending in the proper attitude to the world outside.

The first three are the best known; and they refer to the essential temperament of the individual. Love, joy, peace imply an affectionate, happy, and peaceable disposition.

It will be easier for us to cultivate such a disposition if we remember who it is that is enthroned in our hearts, and let him think his thoughts in us. He, if we let him, will form our temperament and mould our disposition: his sentiments will become more and more truly ours. If we are tempted to think such a suggestion altogether too presumptuous, let us remember that Christ himself prayed that he might dwell in us as the Father dwells in him.

*   *   *

The second trio of virtues consists of those traits of character that are most necessary for the Christian when dealing with other individuals. They are intermediate between one's interior disposition and one's general attitude towards the outside world.

'Long-suffering, gentleness, goodness' is the list as given in our Authorized Version, but each requires re-translation to bring home its meaning in our modern speech. Phillips substitutes 'patience, kindness, generosity'; and he is borne out by the latest lexicon. Here then we have the three most necessary characteristics to bear in mind when we are dealing with other individuals.

We all know that, inasmuch as we are each made in a different mould and no two people can be expected always to see eye to eye with each other, *patience*, including a readiness to listen to another's point of view, is the fundamental requirement in personal contacts. To this must be added *kindness*, in the sense of sympathetic readiness to understand, to put oneself in the other fellow's place. With this must also go an element of *generosity*, a willingness to give the benefit of the doubt, or to concede a point, wherever possible. This pitches the standard rather high, doesn't it? Indeed, it is only attainable, when we already have the loving, happy, peaceable disposition.

*   *   *

The third trio of virtues, the ones that affect our whole attitude to the external world are faithfulness, meekness, temperance. Here again some re-translation is necessary. Faith here means reliability or trustworthiness; the kind of thing you would put in a testimonial to a well-tried servant or officer. Meekness is gentleness, the particular kind of humility we recognize as courtesy. Temperance is in fact the much wider virtue known as self-control: in it there is no room for brashness or self-conceit, but a quiet dignity, knowing the respect that is due to oneself and ready to accord it to others.

Reliable, courteous, dignified—these are not bad traits with which to face the world. We do not need to acquire them. They will grow quite naturally as fruits of the Spirit if we remember that he, who is all perfection, is already truly planted within our hearts.

NO APARTHEID HERE

ST. PAUL was in real trouble over his Galatian converts. After receiving his gospel message and being converted to a simple faith in Christ, they had been enticed to think that there was a better way and had begun to believe that salvation was more sure and more complete if, in addition to Christian observances, one tried to fulfil the demands of the Jewish law.

In his epistle Paul had given a reasoned but passionate assertion of his own teaching; and now, in his eagerness to retain their allegiance to the gospel he had taught, he adds to his secretary's writing a postscript in his own hand. His script could easily be distinguished. Whether he wrote in specially large characters in order that they might be seen and recognized when the letter was held up before the congregation, or whether he did it to emphasize his particular point, or whether he was not so expert as his secretary and wrote in large, childish characters, or whether, as some think, his sight was bad: whatever the reason, he meant to have no mistake about this being identified as his own individual letter.

*   *   *

He was very anxious that his people should not yield to the pressure being put upon them for two reasons, one social, the other psychological. The social reason was that, if they did yield, they would strengthen the barriers that divided humanity. To St. Paul one of the great glories of the Christian faith was precisely that it broke down those barriers. People who were baptized into Christ were made one with him and so with each other.

The fact was that in Christ everyone was made anew. All who owned the faith of Jesus had become a new creation: they were new creatures: they belonged to a new order of existence. Beside such re-creation, matters like circumcision became quite irrelevant. That is why the cross of Christ was the only thing worth boasting about. 'Henceforth let no man trouble me. I am not merely circumcised. I have been crucified with Christ, and for a guarantee you can see the scars of the beatings I have suffered still on my body.'

There was no room for any *apartheid* in a society of people who had had that kind of experience. Whether they had already suffered or not, they had been made new in Christ. Just as pagan devotees sometimes bore the sign of their god cut in the flesh, or as a slave might bear the brand of his master, so Paul bore the visible marks of his Saviour, and his converts bore his invisible sign on their hearts. They were therefore all one in Christ Jesus.

*   *   *

If that was the social reason for Paul's insistence, the psychological reason went deeper still. Basically the question of utmost importance was whether salvation was to be won through an attitude of mind or through the meticulous observance of some rigid code. To St. Paul there was no doubt at all. The only way of salvation was by full and free acceptance of Christ's call. He himself had heard it unmistakably on the Damascus road, and he was sure that everyone else must hear it, if not vividly, at least in such intensity as could not be misunderstood.

This did not mean that such a challenge was once met and was then done with. The voice that spoke to Paul echoed down all the years of his subsequent life. The challenge of Christ is a continuous challenge. The attitude of the Christian is one of continuous attention. Christianity is not just a once-for-all decision, important as that may be, but a continuous life. It is a life in continuous union with Christ, bearing the mark of Christ and recognizing oneself as one of his.

This life will be manifest in our confession of faith, and in the moral standard by which we live. But both will flow from the inward life which Christ shares with us. Here will be no room for superiority or aloofness, but we shall walk together in that peace and enjoy that mercy which are the portion of the Israel of God.

THREE PICTURES

Trinity XVI   *Ephesians 3. 13*

ST. PAUL's profoundest statements are often occasioned by the most simple of local circumstances. To-day's epistle is an example. He is writing to the Ephesians to tell them not to worry because he is imprisoned in Rome. After all, that is really a compliment to them! And then he bursts out into one of the most concentrated and complicated of his transports. As you read it you cannot help being uplifted as you would be by some grand orchestral music, but you can only understand it by pulling it to pieces and carefully analysing it.

The thought of his friends worrying about him drives him to his knees in praise and prayer. The thought of their solidarity with him in the Church fills his mind. Three closely related pictures emerge: the first of a devoted family; the second of a loving community; and the third of a worshipping congregation proclaiming the glory of the divine Father.

*   *   *

First, the Church is a true family because all family relationships spring from God who is the universal Father, and in a special sense the Father of all Christians. The very notion and name of fatherhood are derived from him. He is the source of the family's being: its creator and protector. As the human family looks to its parent for maintenance, so the Church looks instinctively to the Father in heaven for every blessing.

St. Paul prays that the family feeling may be strengthened. That can best be done by recognizing that what

holds the family together in closest unity is the common
Spirit shared by all members. As one blood flows through
the veins of the human family, producing common traits
both physical and psychological in the individual members;
so one Spirit forms the bond of unity for the many
members of the Church. And since that Spirit is the Spirit
of Christ, the features of the Christ-character are repro-
duced in them individually.

*   *   *

The second picture is that of a community not only
beloved but loving. Paul prays that out of the abundant
riches of his own eternal being the Father will strengthen
the Spirit in the hearts of his people, and unite the Church
ever more closely together. But the unity is not a static
condition. It is maintained only at the price of continual
activity, and that is the activity of mutual service.

Later, we find St. John proclaiming quite simply,
'God is Love,' identifying the very nature of highest
Godhead with this activity. St. Paul does not quite reach
that height, but he is here practically saying that *Christ*
is love; and he does in fact imply that to know his love
is to be 'filled with all the fullness of God.'

Here then is a point which cannot be surpassed. Really
to be a member of the loving community and to express
Christ's love in our own lives is to find ourselves one
with all the saints of all the ages, enjoying (incredible as it
may seem) a unity of life with the Supreme Godhead.

*   *   *

The third picture is that of a worshipping congregation.
The activity of mutual love, so characteristic of the happy
family, is not confined to the human circle, but reaches out
in the constant effort to do the highest honour to the head
of the family, to the Father after whom all fatherhood is

named. Like the praises of a great congregation, the lives of those filled and knit together by the Spirit are a continual endeavour to do honour to the God and Father of mankind.

Thus, as we are caught up in the life of the Church and sustained in it by the common energy and force of love, we are lifted beyond the immediate round of mundane concerns. 'Not to worry,' says St. Paul, because all is well with the divine family, in which all are united in community of love and whose innermost life reflects the glory of God.

THE UNITY OF THE SPIRIT

Trinity XVII   *Ephesians* 4. 1

EVERYWHERE there is disunity and everywhere we are looking for a remedy.

In the sphere of international relations we look for something that will hold together East and West. In the Commonwealth we look for something that will replace the old bonds of empire. In the industrial world we seek something to bind together employers and employed in one harmonious body working for one common end. In the Church itself we have a whole ecumenical movement trying to knit together the dislocated limbs of the Body of Christ.

What is this unity of the spirit that St. Paul bids us keep? You will notice that the Prayer Book spells 'spirit' with a small s, thereby suggesting that it is something belonging to the human personality. It can't mean a unity of opinion, for St. Paul would never be so foolish as to expect people all to have the same ideas. There are as many views as there are individuals.

But, as he suggests in another place, if we cannot all have the same opinion we can all have the same mind. We can have a courtesy of the spirit, an inner disposition, that allows to every man the right to differ from ourselves and waits with patience for some way of healing our differences to disclose itself.

*   *   *

And what is this bond of peace in which the unity of the spirit is to be kept? That also is a matter of the disposition. It includes at least two ingredients. It implies

not wanting anything with such overweening desire that
we are determined to get it whatever the cost. It means
also having a common aim so clear before us that we are
prepared to make sacrifices to each other in order to
reach it.

That is what was expected to characterize the councils
of the Church. It was not to be a matter of counting of
heads, of securing a majority vote. When the leaders met
together they were expected to talk things over until the
will of God was made clear to them and they could write
unanimously in their report, 'It seemed good to the Holy
Ghost and to us.' That was the hope with which Con-
stantine and his successors summoned the great Ecumenical
Councils of the early Church. The hope was not always
fulfilled, but that is how we got our creed and definition
of faith.

The bond of peace, then, is the readiness for mutual
accommodation combined with the determination to do
the best for all. In another word it is what the New
Testament means by *agape* or love. If only we could infuse
this positive kind of co-existence into our political and
social life!

*   *   *

Here perhaps we may be helped by noticing that the
more modern English versions spell the word Spirit in
this context with a capital S. They thus imply that the
unity we have to maintain is not that of any ordinary
human disposition but of a divine force or personality.
This seems a more difficult conception, but the New
English Bible comes to our assistance with an entirely fresh
translation. 'Spare no effort to make fast with bonds of
peace the unity which the Spirit gives.'

The unity then that we desire is not something of our
own making. It is nothing less than a gift presented by

the Spirit of God. And that gift is indeed himself. We have to suppose that as a man's whole body is permeated by the influence of his mind, so the whole body of mankind severally and collectively may be permeated by the Spirit of God.

If that is true of the body politic, the State, how much more true must it be of the body ecclesiastic, the Church. We at least must recognize within us the Holy Spirit of God. He is the very quintessence of peace and unity and love. All we have to do is to rest upon his power, allow it to permeate the whole of our individual and corporate being, and express itself in the harmony of our private and public life. There lies the one hope of the world. Lord, how long?

A CAUSE FOR HAPPINESS

ST. PAUL was a man of a naturally happy disposition, of an optimistic, not to say enthusiastic, temperament. We might think that he needed to be all that, in order to stand with fortitude against the many adversities under which he suffered.

No doubt that genial disposition was clouded for a time by the fanaticism that led him into active persecution. His conversion to Christianity offered fresh ground for his confidence and a deeper note of joy began to appear in his letters and speeches. He is not afraid to analyse the sources of his happiness. In to-day's epistle he sees a special cause for it in the manifest advance of his Corinthian converts in the Christian life.

He congratulates them on the free and manifold gifts that God has obviously bestowed upon them. They have assimilated the Christian faith so easily, and show themselves so capable of defending it against all opponents, that they must clearly have been the recipients of God's special trust and favour. This is indeed something to make him devoutly thankful, and he does actually offer heartfelt thanks to God for it on their behalf.

*   *   *

The situation is a particularly happy one for St. Paul, for he has been God's instrument in the conversion of those Corinthians. It was he who had first brought them the good news, and although they were now causing him some of the greatest difficulties of his career, he cannot but be grateful for the privilege of having won them to the faith and seen their quick advance in it.

In a moment he is going to give them warning and serious advice, but just for this paragraph in his letter he lingers over the happiness he has derived from their conversion. What is so splendid is that they have not just been content to take the good news from his lips and accept his account of Christ. They have put it to the test in their own lives and now have the proof of its truth in their own experience.

This is a point of importance in our own day when so many scholars are asking which is the real root of our Christianity, the history of Jesus or the challenge of the eternal Christ? Jesus' teaching in the record of the past or Christ's word to our hearts here and now? St. Paul would have hardly recognized the difference. When he himself had been challenged on the Damascus road he was told that the voice was that of Jesus. It is Christ who speaks to us out of heaven but we know him as the Jesus of history.

Or to put it the other way round: we do not really know the Jesus of history unless we have heard and answered his challenge to us in the present moment. At any rate St. Paul's converts had put his teaching to the trial of their own experience, and it has passed the test triumphantly. Now, says St. Paul, you have everything.

*   *   *

There was, however, another cause for happiness, which is not usually so vivid to us at it was for St. Paul. For him the thought of the end was never long absent. It did not fill him with fear or dismay. It was not a subject to shrink from in polite conversation. It was a pointer to ultimate perfection of happiness, and should therefore be encouraged rather than avoided.

So here the readers are reminded that everything in this world is intended as a preparation for the next.

There is of course no *dogmatic* certainty that they will be faithful to the end. But there is a *moral* certainty. They know that God will be faithful, and they can trust in his Son to strengthen them in all vicissitudes until he leads them safe before the throne of his Father.

Our final end is not a question of theological debate but of personal relations. Our ultimate future is not determined by logic but by the love God bears towards us. If we trust him he will 'confirm us unto the end that we may be blameless in the day of our Lord Jesus Christ.' You can always depend upon God. That is the real cause for St. Paul's happiness and for ours.

CHANGING STEP

WHAT is most important about a man is his general attitude to life. Even if you are interviewing a would-be office boy, the questions you ask him are only significant in so far as they enable you to glimpse something of the boy's general character and his probable attitude to you and the job. It is that initial approach on his part that will dictate the whole course of his conduct.

Our epistle is concerned precisely with this general approach. St. Paul thinks our attitude of mind all-important. If that is right we start off on the right foot in life, but if it is wrong we are likely to be out of step all the time. What is specially interesting in Paul is that he is so very optimistic about our chances of changing step if we have been wrong.

He has no hesitation in describing the wrong attitude as that of the Gentiles; that is, the people outside the sphere of revealed religion altogether. It was characterized by two features, ignorance and vanity. They did not know what life was all about, and so they followed the emptiest of pursuits: their life was void of purpose and utterly wasted.

It was because of this essential emptiness of their lives, with nothing to aim at and nothing to look forward to, that they gave themselves up to evil courses. That there was much that was noble in ancient life we need not doubt, but that its character as a whole merited St. Paul's strictures many moralists have agreed.

*   *   *

Then comes the equally vivid description of the change. 'But ye have not so learned Christ.' Your contact with him has given you an entirely different point of view as a result of which you threw off that old manner of life as if you were stripping off dirty linen.

The fact is that you have been 'renewed in the spirit of your mind.' Your whole outlook on life has been changed; an entirely fresh attitude has been created for you. 'The spirit of your mind' is an extraordinary expression, implying the very quintessential character and tone of personality, in other words the disposition. It is our innermost disposition that is the keynote to our character and is likely to dictate our whole code of conduct.

Consequently if we have the right disposition we shall be like people who have put on a fresh, clean set of inner clothing. We shall be newly invigorated and our outward demeanour will express our inward frame of mind. Instead of ignorance and vanity leading to evil courses there will be in us the 'new man' full of hope and purpose, living a life of righteousness and true holiness.

* * *

All this happens because we are now joined with the Holy Spirit of God. He who is Christ's 'other self' is, so to speak, resident within us, and as we yield ourselves to his dictation he will enable us to live out our lives according to God's will. That should make things easy, but human nature being what it is we are prone to let the old habits creep back again.

St. Paul, who is never inclined to leave anything to chance, gets down to bed-rock and gives us a double list, one of the things we are to avoid, and the other of the things we are actually to do. It is surprising what things he has to warn his Ephesian converts against—lying and thieving, as well as anger and loose talk. These are the

L

people whom at the opening of his epistle he called 'saints.' We can realize how strongly even in their case the old habits might try to reassert themselves.

But St. Paul is not prepared to leave a vacuum. In place of those vanities life should be filled with positive good. Truth, hard work, kindness to one another, and a real desire in our daily conversation to help one another— that is what should come naturally to us.

If we contrast the two pictures 'before' and 'after,' we shall realize the extent of the change.

RECIPE FOR HAPPINESS

Trinity XX   *Ephesians* 5. 15

IN to-day's Epistle St. Paul gives us a prescription for a good and happy life. It has three ingredients, three rules of conduct. First, he says in effect, be careful; then be cheerful; and third, give thought to others.

First, then, we are to be careful. 'Walk circumspectly.' We are not to be like the foolish people who have no thought except for the pleasure of the moment. In such engrossment opportunity steals upon us unawares and it has passed us by before we are conscious of its presence. We are to 'redeem the time,' that is to buy up the opportunity, let no chance slip. And when you have caught it, use it to the full.

Our care must also be exercised in seeing that we do not run into any kind of excess. Our guide must not be our own desire or emotion but the will of God. We must try earnestly to find out what his will for us is, and then endeavour to fulfil it.

If we are seriously aiming at doing his will we shall find it much easier to stop short of intemperance of every kind, whether food, drink, thought or speech, than if we are mere slaves to the incitement of the moment. Recognizing the Lord's purpose behind the ordinary circumstances of everyday life we shall concentrate our energies on getting it done, rather than satisfying our own immoderate desires.

*   *   *

There is, however, one kind of intoxication that is commendable in the Christian, and that is enthusiasm in the service of God. This enthusiasm should be so

strongly felt that it lifts us out of the rut of commonplace
tastes and fills all our waking moments with the happiness
of knowing that we are doing with our life precisely what
we are intended to do.

We have, in other words, to cultivate a happy disposition. What is needed is no forced cheerfulness but the
natural zest for life of a contented and successful person.
Our success need not necessarily be what the world calls
by that name: it is sufficient to know that we are doing
the will of God.

St. Paul can find no better way of describing that kind
of disposition than by saying that it is as if our hearts were
filled with music. It is the happiness of the boy who goes
whistling on his way, of the girl who finds herself humming
under her breath as she works about the home. It is the
evidence of a contented mind, of a heart that for the
moment at least is at peace with itself and the world.

This is what it means to be 'filled with the Spirit.'
For the Christian this disposition is not the fruit of some
passing condition. It is a permanent set of the mind
secure in the consciousness of the life of Christ flooding
one's soul and setting the whole of one's existence along
the line of his purposes.

*   *   *

Be careful, be cheerful: these may be merely self-
regarding virtues. They are saved from falling into selfish-
ness by the final injunction, 'Submit yourselves one to
another in the fear of God.' If we really are intent on
doing the will of God, then we shall remember the example
of Christ and his devotion to his fellow-men.

We shall not walk rough-shod over the ways of life,
trampling on others and failing to have regard for their
feelings. We shall have the true gentleman's sensitiveness
to the tastes, to the involuntary likes and dislikes of others,

and we shall have the courtesy to accommodate ourselves to them as far as possible.

More positively we shall be ready to defer to one another, not just as a matter of form, a mere trick of politeness—good as that may be—but in a real desire to let everyone have just what they want.

Society is not a mere congeries of individuals. It is a well-knit organism, of which each human being is a living member. The body as a whole thrives only when the needs of each member are adequately satisfied. Here is plenty of room for being careful and for manifesting a cheerful spirit. Such efforts will not only assist our care for others: they will vastly increase our own pleasure in life.

THE CHRISTIAN STAND

THE second generation of Christians felt themselves
uneasily poised between two overwhelmingly important points of time, the first coming of Christ and the
second. They had in large part forgotten the rapture of
the first coming, and the second was so delayed that there
was no longer any excitement in the expectation.

The evangelists had to meet the sensation of flatness that
resulted. In the Fourth Gospel the emphasis is laid on
eternity, and the readers are encouraged to see the
incidents that take place in time as reflections of what is
always true in the eternal sphere. This lesson is brought
out even in the way St. John recounts the healing of the
nobleman's son. Time and distance are no object to Jesus.
He does not need to see the boy: he just announces his
healing, and at the very moment the patient began to
recover. Christ's saving power is independent of time and
space. It belongs to eternity.

The faith of the nobleman consisted in the fact that he
was ready to accept this situation. He did not ask for any
'sign' to justify his trust in Jesus. The only thing he was
anxious about was that the Healer should get on with his
beneficent work. He must not argue, but use his power at
once. Jesus answers in effect that it is done. There is no
chronological sequence of events. The miracle reveals
that instantaneousness which is the mark of eternity.

*   *   *

It is not fanciful to see, in the epistle, St. Paul teaching
the same lesson in his own way. The emphasis is not on a
series of encounters between opposing champions (though

such there must be), but on the continuous stand made by
the Christian warrior. The abiding, all-at-once character
of eternity is reflected in the steadfastness of the soldier of
Christ.

The picture is that of the heavy-armed infantryman
of the Roman army, whose main duty is to withstand the
shock of opposing troops. If he is shod in such a way as to
allow for agility in movement, his main defensive weapon
is the great shield covered with leather with which he
can catch the arrows tipped with fire that are despatched
by an enemy hoping to create confusion and panic in
his ranks.

But indeed he is fully armed and prepared for any
eventuality. His essential function is to stand fast, and
still to remain standing when the enemy has exhausted
all his skill and courage against him. Eternity is reflected
in this character of the Christian soldier.

After all, that is the sphere to which he properly belongs.
He is to maintain his contact with it through prayer,
praying always, with all perseverance, continually remembering his leaders and his comrades before God. Even this
state of prayer is not merely a series of separate acts, but
the whole set of a mind that is permanently stayed on God.

*   *   *

It goes without saying that such a condition is more
easily described than achieved. Yet it has been expected
of each succeeding generation of Christians. The collect
points us to the way in which we, in our turn, can acquire
this steadfastness and secure this continuity in our own
lives. It can only be done by a mind that is at peace.

Such peace comes in three stages: through the knowledge of the pardon by which God takes us into fellowship
with himself: through the deliberate effort to be rid of
the sin that would erect a fresh barrier between ourselves

and God; and through the quietness that comes from the continuous sense of his presence.

The Christian who is thus fortified is, like the heavy-armed soldier, strengthened to resist the occasional but repeated shocks of the enemy. His penitence is not just the reiterated confession of sinful acts, but the whole consciousness of a personality that feels itself empty if it is not filled with the reality of God.

It is this continual presence and our steadfast recollection of it that lifts us above the storms and chances of this temporal world. That events, good and bad, will happen to us in time we are fully aware, but they will be powerless to throw us into panic or dislodge us from our stand.

THE IDEAL CHARACTER

THE relation between St. Paul and the Philippians was close to the point of intimacy. It was not that merely of a leader with his followers, of an apostle with his disciples, it was that of friend with friend. St. Paul says that no one has been so good to him as the Philippians, and he writes to tell them how grateful he is.

Out of this expression of thanks there springs a description of the hopes he entertains for their future development. And this leads him to an almost accidental analysis of the ideal Christian character. What sort of person ought the good Christian to be? The fact that the answer is given so incidentally makes it all the more intriguing.

Of course everything is grounded in love. That is taken for granted. Out of that love springs the first pair of necessary graces, knowledge and judgment.

This is particularly interesting, since there was at that time a growing dispute as to the importance of knowledge. Indeed the necessity of knowledge was already being over-stressed to the point where it became a heresy. St. Paul does not go so far as that. He does not claim that knowledge by itself can bring salvation, but he does claim that it is of great value where it may be had, and that it is our duty as well as our privilege to add to it as far as we can.

*   *   *

But knowledge without judgment can be a snare and a delusion. We do not need only to have our storehouse full: we need to know how to apply and use the stores we have obtained.

This is the second point in Paul's ideal character, the gift of true discrimination, so that we may 'give approval to the best things.' The marginal translation in the New English Bible suggests, 'may teach you by experience what things are most worth while.'

What the Greek really implies is the faculty of noticing and appreciating the things that are different, the things of special excellence. Here again it is interesting to see how St. Paul, rabbinical Jew that he was, had nevertheless imbibed a good deal of the Greek spirit from his surroundings. The Greeks not only set great store by knowledge; they were also phenomenally quick to notice anything particularly beautiful or striking, or of specially high quality in any sphere.

That is a good trait, and the Christian should copy it. It is easy enough to criticize and find fault. Some people do it so much that there is hardly any word of praise left in their vocabulary. The Christian's task is not so negative. He has a positive duty to perform. He must be constantly on the look-out for something he can genuinely praise, for something really worth while.

*   *   *

Knowledge, discrimination: to these must be added as a third element in the ideal character the effort to be 'sincere and without offence.' One sticks to the old translation 'sincere,' although such others have been proposed as 'perfect,' 'flawless.'

Perhaps the latter gives a clue. You send a ring to be cleaned, and when the jeweller returns it he says you ought to know that there is a flaw in the principal gem. It had been there all the time, and your ring was less valuable than you thought. You cannot help feeling a certain disappointment. You would not wish your own character to be like that.

Sincerity indeed is the very foundation of true religion. There cannot be true religion without it. We cannot deceive God; then why should we deceive ourselves or others? We must learn to look into our own hearts and see ourselves as God sees us. We must try to be utterly sincere with ourselves as we inevitably are with God.

Knowledge, discrimination, sincerity. If they can become true of us, we shall have the opportunity of yielding to him 'the full harvest of righteousness,' which comes not through our own unaided efforts, but through Jesus Christ to the glory and praise of God.

CITIZENSHIP WITH THE SAINTS

THE Greek word for a witness is martyr. This fact should be sufficient to assure us that the invisible hosts who throng the spiritual area are not mere spectators. They are the Chataways of the heavenly contest: they have themselves been competitors, they have won their event, and they now crowd the stands to comfort us by their presence and to cheer us on while we in our turn engage in the continual struggle.

We have not been altogether kind to these many heroes of the Christian warfare. Only too often they have been half forgotten, and we have not even troubled to keep our list of the greatest of them complete. In England our official calendar is singularly deficient in modern saints. But the neglect is to be remedied. Since the last Lambeth Conference, the local churches have been encouraged to observe the anniversaries of their own particular heroes in addition to those already on the universally accepted list. In due course, it is felt, the mind of the Church will single out those whose outstanding witness demands the widest possible recognition. It will be interesting to see in days to come what a large proportion of the names thus singled out will belong to the younger churches overseas.

*   *   *

It is perhaps inevitable that in such a context we should think first of heroism and courage of a physical kind. After all, that is the easiest standard of measurement. But it is by no means the sole distinguishing mark of the saint. Indeed it may be only by the special grace of

God, and not by any natural endowment, that the saint can show any physical courage at all.

The distinguishing mark of the saint is his preoccupation with the thought of God. God indeed is in all his thoughts: he endures as seeing him who is invisible. For most of us a real effort is required to part, even for a second, the veil of material things and to penetrate the unseen. To the few the capacity appears to come naturally and without struggle. Readers of Evelyn Underhill's life will remember how almost terrifying was her calm and apparently constant sense of the presence of God. For the saints, to maintain contact with God is the most precious thing in life: beside it everything else falls into insignificance.

The other great characteristic of the saint is his passion for holiness. His is not the moderate and respectable morality that appeals to the rest of us, but the ardent, glowing virtue that rejoices in great sacrifices and thrives on opposition. In our Church of England this was the characteristic note of the lives of such diverse teachers as Wesley and Simeon, Newman and Pusey.

*   *   *

We are not to suppose that those who have fought the good fight and gone to their reward are now simply spectators of the continuing struggle. They do not merely sit around the arena and watch us from a distance. They are closer to us than ever they were in mortal life. We speak of the 'communion of saints,' and that means something more even than close fellowship.

All Christians are 'in Christ.' His is a universal personality. In it those who are 'grafted into him' have a share, as the grafted twig has a share in the life of the tree into which it grows. If we are thus incorporated into one common life there must be a sense in which we are incorporated into each other. The nearer we are to him, the nearer shall we be to one another, just as the radii of a circle draw nearer to each other as they proceed from the circumference until they finally mingle in the centre.

All this great array of the saints, known and unknown, is not an alien society, not an *elite*, with whom we have only a remote connection. In some mysterious way their life has flowed into ours. We belong to their company: our place is in their ranks: we are one with them. We cannot betray them or let them down. We rely on our Leader to make us like them.

REMEMBRANCE SUNDAY

Trinity XXIV   *Colossians* 1. 3

DO the dead heroes whom we commemorate on Remembrance Day witness the impressive scene in Whitehall, and are they conscious of the thousands of annual services held in their honour throughout the country? If so, does the fact that they are so remembered bring them some added compensation for the sacrifice they made?

Maeterlinck, in his play, *Blue Bird*, has a scene in which the children, searching for happiness, penetrate into the land of memory, where their departed grandparents are resting completely unconscious in the dust and cobwebs of forgetfulness. It is only when the children remember them and seek them out that the old people come to life at all.

As it stands, that is a mere piece of pagan sentimentalism. But with a little extension it can easily be brought into line with the Christian belief in the communion of saints. We hold that those who are in the bosom of the Father are always conscious and live in a condition of life greatly enhanced above anything that we know on earth. But we may well believe that there is a quickening of their joy when they know themselves remembered on earth.

*   *   *

That is a thought that is inevitably brought to our mind by the observance of this day. And there are others. Can we go through these commemorative services without groaning once again at the appalling wastage of human life involved in two world wars? Is it possible that man can set so little value on this most fundamental of God's gifts—that of existence?

One remembers a discussion with some members of the Russian Orthodox community, in which the speakers were trying to analyse the difference between the Russian and the English mentality. A particularly intelligent and devout member of the Orthodox party said she thought the basic difference lies in the emphasis the English put on the mere fact of living. The Russian temperament set much less store by the physical reality of life and was therefore much more ready to surrender it when the need arose.

In sharp contrast to that view one thinks of Schweitzer building his whole philosophy on the irreplaceable value of life, and, great physician and surgeon that he was, regretting the necessity that forced him to destroy even the lowest form of life, the germs that bring disease.

Somewhere between these two extremes lies the essentially Christian view, accepting life as a sacred and supreme gift from God to be guarded by all the skill available, and relying on the knowledge that, when it leaves the temporal sphere, it is not thus lost but flowers into a new glory in life eternal.

*   *   *

Another thought that arises unbidden but none the less cogent on this annual occasion is that of the obligation under which we rest towards those whom we honour on this day. If we have 'never had it so good,' it is to them that we owe the opportunity of affluence and ease.

At the lowest estimate this must involve us in a great debt of gratitude. But it surely involves us in much more than that. In every sphere of society we have repeatedly had to recognize how much the world has lost through this wholesale destruction of so large a proportion of its finest manhood in one generation. We should not be doing our duty to our dead if we did not strive our utmost to take their place, to pick up where they left off, and as far as possible to do the work they would have done, as well as our own.

We do not show our gratitude to them merely by enjoying the privileges they have won for us, but by striving to carry on the struggle where they were compelled to lay it down. We have scripture warrant for believing that they are witnesses of our efforts; they are spectators around the arena; they cheer us on; and the knowledge of their presence should be one of the greatest incentives to us who inherit their task.

THE NATURE OF GOD'S LOVE

Trinity XXV   1 *St. John* 3. 1

WE often speak of the love of God: we do not often ask what kind of love it is. The question is forced on us this week when we fill in a vacant Sunday after Trinity with the 'proper' from Epiphany VI.

The epistle both puts the question and answers it. It tells three descriptive facts about the Father's love for his children: it is adoptive: it is purgative: it is unitive.

First, it is adoptive. It is like the love of foster-parents for the child they have adopted into their own family and which they treat as if it were part of their own flesh and blood. Adoption has become so common a feature of the social life of our day that we need little effort to understand the emotions it arouses. But there are thousands of couples who without it might have lived childless all their days, and there are thousands who without it might never have known the secure background of a home and parental affection.

By thus adopting us and calling us his sons, God has bridged the gap between himself and the universe he has made. He has taken us out of a world that had become hostile to him and brought us within the fellowship of his own home.

*　　　*　　　*

But this does not mean that God's love is indulgent. It is not the doting sentiment a fond parent may feel for a favourite child. There is indeed no sentimentality about it at all. God knows our capabilities and expects the best of us.

Nothing less can befit the children of God. They must behave as members of his household.

Home is the best training-ground of character, because it is normally there that we are shown understanding and sympathy without indulgence. A man's wife and children are his best critics because they know him so well and are so fond of him. Perfect love casts out fear; we are not afraid in the family to speak the truth; but we speak it in love.

Love does not blind us to sin, or teach us to call it by some other name. We do not make excuses for one another unless they are deserved. The child of God, like any other child, knows that the respect of his family is worth having, and so he seeks to purify himself even as Christ is pure.

*   *   *

The love of God, then, is first adoptive and then purgative. He first calls us his sons and then expects us to behave as such, purging out the old sinful habits and acquiring the kind of character that is proper to a son of God.

It is there that we begin to feel uncertain. We are happy that God should honour us by taking us into the select circle of his family: we recognize that we must try to live up to the standards of that family: but what guarantee have we that we shall be able to do so? What we are mostly conscious of is our weakness and failure. Where can we find any sort of security that we shall even remotely approximate to the divine standard?

This is where the third feature of God's love applies. It is unitive. Like all true love it desires union with its object. God is not content with making us his sons: he makes us partakers of his own being. This he does through our unity with his Son, who has already taken our nature upon him. Although we have never seen him, he dwells in us and we in him. We can feel the influence of his presence in our lives.

And how can we detect that influence? By the readiness with which we begin to want to help one another. Love is a practical thing: it is not a mere sentiment. The real test is whether we try to do deeds of helpfulness.

This is what transforms us. We do not know what we shall be, but we shall be like him. The ultimate vision of God and the full realization of what his love means will complete the change in us. Herein is God's love made perfect, brought to its full consummation, if we love one another.

AN IDYLLIC FUTURE

JEREMIAH is often described as the prophet of gloom, but in to-day's epistle he is anything but gloomy. He paints for his people an idyllic future.

He uses the method of typology, which regards certain past events of Israel's history as animated pictures of what is to happen with increased significance in the more or less distant future. Thus, while his people are divided, many of them in exile, and all alike suffering under the dominance of a foreign power, he bids them look back to the reign of their great model king, David. What he did in the past shall be done again; the dismembered tribes of Israel and Judah shall be restored to their former unity; they will live together in peace and safety; and prosperity will be a characteristic feature of their new life.

*   *   *

But that would not be the only, or even the most important, characteristic of the new reign. The very name of the scion of the house of David who would bring the deliverance would indicate that. He would be called the 'Lord our Righteousness,' that is, 'the Lord himself is righteousness and he will do right by us.'

Now that was the very name borne by the last, de-throned King of Judah, Zedekiah, for whom no one could have anything but pity—he was so feeble a king and suffered so cruelly at the hands of his conquerors. But the new King, bearing that name, would redeem it from ignominy: he would deliver his people from the contemporary enemies coming down from the north by the Fertile Crescent, just as in the old days Moses had delivered his people from the southern enemies in the land of Egypt. The deliverance from Egypt would turn out to be a 'type' fulfilled in the new deliverance from Babylon.

In this way the new King would execute judgment. Amos had long ago warned both Israel and Judah that, just because God was righteous, his judgment, when it came, would fall on all that was evil, whether within the chosen people or outside: the Hebrews could expect no privileged position at the bar of justice. But now, surely, they had been punished enough. First Israel and then Judah had been carried away captive. If God's justice was to be executed on this earth by God's agent, then it *must* be part of the duty of the coming King to 'restore the Kingdom to Israel.'

*   *   *

The echo of this phrase from the New Testament reminds us that a later generation looked for the fulfilment of this prophecy in the work of Jesus of Nazareth. There is good reason to believe that Jesus himself recognized in this kind of teaching a forecast of his mission. No doubt he stripped the expectation of its grosser associations with the profession of arms and the exercise of violence. Nevertheless he did not entirely repudiate all the suggestions of a material prosperity.

That is surely part, at least, of the purport of to-day's gospel. The feeding of the five thousand is a graphic illustration of the prosperity that would attend the establishment of the Kingdom of God on earth. That indeed did not exhaust its significance. The very chapter of St. John from which our passage is taken goes on to associate the bread thus given to the multitude with the Bread of Life, the manna that fell from heaven, and so with the flesh of

Christ; and there is no doubt that the congregation for
whom the Fourth Gospel was written would associate
that food with the Bread of the Eucharist.

*   *   *

So we go from the delivery from Egypt and the Red
Sea to the delivery from Babylon; and from the delivery
from Babylon to the delivery from sin and the powers
of evil. And always God provides adequate sustenance
for his people. He is the Lord our Righteousness. His
judgment can be relied upon, and in the end he always
manifests it in the same way, by delivering his people
from their sins and providing them with a new and richer
life.